One *of* thousands, this book is donated to the Roesch Library by Laila and Robert Werner, a graduate *of* the class *of* 1936

*This gift is dedicated
to the memory of
Robert Reiling,
a classmate and dear friend*

"A good book is the precious lifeblood of a master spirit, embalmed and treasured up on purpose to a life beyond life." — *Milton*

CHILDREN
OF
POVERTY

STUDIES ON THE EFFECTS
OF SINGLE PARENTHOOD,
THE FEMINIZATION OF POVERTY,
AND HOMELESSNESS

edited by
STUART BRUCHEY
UNIVERSITY OF MAINE

A GARLAND SERIES

MIDDLE-AGED, FEMALE AND HOMELESS

The Stories of a Forgotten Group

SANDRA S. BUTLER

GARLAND PUBLISHING, INC.
NEW YORK & LONDON / 1994

Copyright © 1994 by Sandra S. Butler
All rights reserved

Library of Congress Cataloging-in-Publication Data

Butler, Sandra S., 1957–
    Middle-aged, female and homeless : the stories of a forgotten group / Sandra S. Butler.
       p. cm. — (Children of poverty)
    Includes bibliographical references and index.
    ISBN 0–8153–1544–9 (alk. paper)
    1. Homeless women—United States. 2. Homelessness—United States. 3. Shelters for the homeless—United States. I. Title. II. Series.
HV4505.B9 1994
362.83'08'6942—dc20
                            93-34143
                            CIP

Printed on acid-free, 250-year-life paper
Manufactured in the United States of America

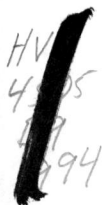

This book is dedicated to people all over the world who do not have permanent homes of their own.

CONTENTS

Dedication v
Table of contents vii
Preface xi
Acknowledgments xix
Introduction xxi
Chapter 1: Literature Review 1
   Homelessness: General Overview 1
      Causes of Homelessness 1
         Economic conditions 2
         Low-income housing availability 5
         Deinstitutionalization of the mentally ill 7
         Substance abuse and domestic violence 8
      Services to the Homeless 8
      Public Responses to the Homeless 11
   Homeless Women/Female Poverty at Midlife 12
      Homeless Women 12
      Impoverished Middle-aged Women 18
   Conclusion 19
Chapter 2: Method 21
   Introduction 21
   Research Goals and Questions 21
   Overall Methodological Approach 23
   Interviews with Homeless Women 26
      Sample Selection and Shelter Description 26
         Criteria for being in sample 26
         Selecting shelters 26
         Downtown Emergency Services Center 27
         Lutheran Compass Center 27
         Angeline's 28
         Winter Women's Shelter 28
      Recruitment 28

Staying in Contact with my Sample 29
Attrition 31
Interview Questions, Taping and Transcribing 31
Procedures of Analysis 33
Reliability and Validity..................................34
Limitations 35
Interviews with Service Providers 36
Sample Selection 36
Interview Questions 37
Procedures of Analysis 37
Observation 37
Protection of Human Subjects 39
Table 1--Frequency of Interviews 40
Chapter 3: Sample Description 41
Introduction 41
Sample Description 41
Introduction to Findings Chapters 44
Chapter 4: Pathways to Homelessness 47
Introduction 47
Relationships 48
Resiliency 51
Normalcy 57
Political Awareness 60
Chapter 5: Day to Day Lives 65
Introduction 65
Relationships 66
Resiliency 72
Normalcy 78
Political Awareness 82
Chapter 6: Plans and Hopes for the Future 87
Introduction..87
Relationships 87
Resiliency 94
Normalcy 98
Political Awareness 102
Chapter 7: Services for Homeless Women 109
Introduction 109
What the Women Said 109
Use and Opinions of Shelters and Drop-in Center 109

Table of Contents

    Different Reactions to Services 111
    What the Service Providers Said 113
Chapter 8: Discussion and Policy Implications 117
    Introduction 117
    Themes from Data 118
        Relationships... 118
        Resiliency 121
        Normalcy 122
        Political Awareness 123
    Services for Homeless Women: What the Providers
        and Consumers Say 124
    Policy Implications 127
        Housing 128
        Income Maintenance 129
        Employment/Education and Training 131
        Health 132
        Nutrition 132
    Future Research 133
    My Personal Reactions to this Research Experience ... 135
    Conclusion 137
References 139
Index 149

PREFACE

It has been over two years since I finished data collection for this study--since I stopped riding buses each day down to downtown Seattle to meet the women whose stories fill the following pages. I think of these women often and have heard from several of them through letters, but my life has clearly moved away from theirs. I often wonder about the injustice of this world that allowed me--the researcher--to enter into the lives of these eleven women for six months, to learn from them, be changed by them, and then to leave. While doing the interviews from September 1990 to March 1991, I would leave the street each evening to return to the comfort of my apartment and bed, and in August 1991, I left Seattle altogether to begin an academic job on the other side of the country.

While conducting the research on these women's lives, I struggled with the conflict with which many feminist researchers do battle? Was I merely a voyeur and one more cog in the oppressive wheel that rolled over these women's lives on a daily basis? Or was there some value in telling the stories of a forgotten group--telling their stories as they told them to me? I have not solved this conflict; it still troubles me. But I have learned over the past two years, as I have reported on these findings to my friends, students, conference participants, or anyone who happens to be interested, that certain stereotypes of homeless women are alive and well. Policies and programs aimed at improving the quality of life of homeless women and other oppressed populations will be more effective if based on accurate information, not myths and speculations. This study does a small part in meeting that need.

In the two years since my own investigation two seminal books on homeless women have been published. *The Women Outside* (1992), by Stephanie Golden, and *Tell Them Who I Am* (1993), by Elliot Liebow. Both books grew out of the experiences of the authors in their years of being volunteers in shelters for homeless women. While I found both of the books to be thoughtful, sensitive and informative, I am struck by the fact that while we continue to research and publish, the rate of homelessness increases unabated. Women now make up fifty percent of the homeless population (Brown & Ziefert, 1990; Sullivan, 1991). While there was an initial high from the 1992 presidential elections--a hope that 12 years of neglect and attack on social programs would be arrested and turned around--expectations for truly progressive reforms have been moderated as the Clinton administration responds increasingly to its more conservative constituency. Neither increasing the stock of low-income housing nor making public assistance more available and generous are government priorities in this time of economic recession and deficit preoccupation. Clearly, each of these books would be very worthwhile reading for current policy makers.

Golden is a freelance journalist who volunteered for several years at a Manhattan shelter for women. She goes well beyond describing the lives of the women she meets to exploring the historical roots and mythology surrounding "deviant" women--a category in which homeless women fit. She theorizes that society has cast the homeless woman--the bag lady--as our modern witch. Homeless women are existing on the edge of conventional society and are thus threatening to all of us. In an article published before her book, and on which she expands in *The Women Outside*, she submits that we do not know how to categorize homeless women:

> Whereas a homeless man fits comfortably into a variety of categories (hobo, tramp, bum, vagrant), a homeless woman evokes intense discomfort. Women have always been defined so entirely in terms of whom they belong to that no category exists for a woman without family or home. If one thinks of society as a pattern of social forms that create categories into which its members fit, such a woman must be marginal, in the sense that because she fits into the pattern nowhere she has to exist at its edge. (Golden, 1990, p. 1)

Golden's work provides us with an important and provocative feminist analysis of society's treatment of homeless women.

Liebow is a renowned anthropologist, known particularly for his 1967 study of African American street corner life, *Tally's Corner*. He brings the same skill and sensitivity used in his earlier work to the participant observer study of homeless women, *Tell Them Who I Am*. His data come from over four years of volunteer work at a shelter for

Preface   *xiii*

homeless women in the Washington DC area. His research uncovered themes similar to those I discovered in my own data, in particular the themes of relationships, normalcy and resiliency. He includes the stories of nearly fifty women with whom he had contact over the years. He describes their exterior day to day lives, but also reaches into their souls to try to understand what allows these women to survive in the face of such adversity. Liebow emphasizes the diversity of the women--once again debunking myths and stereotypes. The main unifying characteristic of this group was the fact that they had no home; their path to homelessness almost always had to do with being poor and powerless.

> Seen from a distance, the women appeared to be a fairly homogeneous group. They were mainly from lower working-class and lower-class families. With few exceptions, they were poor and did not have many marketable skills beyond domestic and clerical work. But as one moved closer to the women--close enough to see them as individuals--they appeared to be strikingly different from one another, more different perhaps than their more successful non-homeless counterparts. (Liebow, 1993, p. 16)

The homeless women described in these two books ranged in age from young adult to elderly. As a group, homeless people are getting younger. The median age of homeless people today is 34 years, 20 years younger than was true two decades ago (Kutza & Keigher, 1991). But the number of middle-aged and elderly homeless individuals is not insignificant and continues to increase. Sullivan (1991) reminds us that homeless women--and particularly older homeless women--have been largely ignored despite their increasing numbers:

> The homeless population is becoming younger and women tend to be younger than men. However, there is a sizable number of older homeless women. Garrett and Bahr, in their 1973 study found that the mean age for homeless women was 47 years compared to a mean age of 54 years for men. In a later survey, their data revealed that 24% of the homeless women they studied were age 55 and over, the second largest group: 10% were age 65 and over 14% were ages 55 to 64. A

more recent survey of the New York City shelter population revealed that 18% of the women and 12% of the male residents were age 50 and over. Just as women were a hidden sub-group of the homeless, the elderly remain a hidden sub-population of homeless women. (Sullivan, 1991, p. 7)

I submit that middle-aged homeless women are even more hidden than the elderly; programs, services and public sympathy are more likely to be directed at the elderly than the middle-aged. Poor women at mid-life are a neglected and invisible population in our country (Butler & Weatherley, 1992). While being without a home is a tragedy for anyone no matter what age or sex, some of the short-term and long-term solutions to this social problem may be different for different subgroups among the homeless. As Benda and Dattalo (1990) point out:

> Without some systematic means of distinguishing the various subgroups, theory and practice tend to be biases toward certain subgroups and to ignore others. (p. 51)

Not only do middle-aged homeless women require different emergency services once they are on the streets, but their pathways to homelessness are particular to their sex and age. As stated in a report to the Select Committee on Aging (1980):

> The world that mid-life women face is the same unequal world that all women face. But the inequalities are more severe for mid-life women because of two reasons:
> --They are less equipped to overcome these inequities than are their more broadly educated and socialized young adult daughters;
> --The built-in rigidities of society are especially restrictive in the older years. (pp. 4-5)

The structural interventions that will be necessary to slow the rate of impoverishment and eventually homelessness of women were not ignored in the special volume on homelessness published by the American Psychological Association in November, 1991. While the article on homeless women (Milburn & D'Ercole, 1991) in this volume used a rather traditional psychological approach--a stress model--to examine the experience of homelessness for women, the authors concluded by saying that interventions need to be systematic rather than individualistic.

> Critical components of the solution to homelessness include a viable public education system, decent living wages with health and child care benefits for all workers, and greater awareness of the ethnic, racial, gender, and cultural diversity of American society and the growing economic need to no longer relegate ethnic and racial minorities and women to the bottom rungs of our society. (p. 1168)

While there has been a marked increase in literature on homeless women in the past two years, there has been an even greater increase in the number of books and scholarly articles on homelessness in general. I will not review them all here, as I am probably unaware of many; no doubt an important book on homelessness is coming off the press as I write this preface. Once again, the quantity of literature we are producing, when weighed against our inability to create a just society, is disquieting; the link between good analysis and good policy is not always a direct one. No doubt this is due in large part to the fairly dramatic reforms for which some authors call; reforms that may be inconsistent with the values of our patriarchal, capitalist society. Barak (1991), for example, in his book *Gimme Shelter* emphasizes that until we as a country are willing to face our injustices, we will not solve the problem of homelessness. He places the blame for homelessness on the class structure of our capitalist state, and believes solutions to this social problem rest in fundamental changes in our political economy.

Baum and Burns (1993) on the other hand take a more individualistic approach which is a less threatening analysis to the status quo. In their book *A Nation in Denial*, these authors place blame on advocates for minimizing the problems of substance abuse and mental illness; they believe advocates have been deceiving themselves about the causes of homelessness. According to Baum and Burns, by emphasizing structural causes, advocates are standing in the way of solving the social problem of homelessness.

> In marked contrast to many current analysts of homelessness, we do not consider major social, economic, and political

> forces to be at the root of today's homelessness. Inadequate housing, poverty, unemployment, declining social benefits, and governmental cutbacks have disastrous consequences for the poor and disadvantaged of America, but the homeless suffer from more immediate problems that prevent them from maintaining themselves in stable housing, from working, and from utilizing social benefits. If left untreated, these problems lead to isolation and alienation, misery, serious physical health problems, and early death. The effects of alcoholism, drug addiction, and/or mental illness are the precipitating cause of the downward spiral that ends with the disconnection from a society that stigmatizes the people who suffer from these diseases. (p.170).

I cannot support the thesis of these authors, though I applaud their attempts to destigmatize substance abuse and mental illness. While some of the women described in this study did in fact suffer from substance abuse or periods of mental illness, and each of these women would have benefited from more accessible treatment, I do not believe that their ongoing homelessness was "caused" by these factors. People with more resources, access to medical care and benefits, or in more privileged positions in our society also deal with substance abuse and mental illness but tend to remain housed. Without a doubt we cannot ignore the need for accessible treatment as a part of our response to this problem, but I include myself with the advocates these authors discredit in saying that substance abuse and mental illness are not *the cause* of homelessness.

In contrast, Blau (1992) provides a more structural analysis of the causes of homelessness in his book *The Visible Poor*. He gives a very thorough and up-to-date discussion of the effects of economic transformation and deindustrialization, cutbacks in social welfare and our lack of commitment as a nation to provide sufficient low-income housing. After examining the inadequacy of our current responses to homelessness, he puts forth his own ideas for economic and social welfare reforms that would be better able to meet common human needs. Perhaps because I share his discipline social work--I found Blau's analysis and solutions to be particularly appealing and most in line with my own thinking; his list of policy reforms are along the same lines as those suggested in this study. Additionally, as I promote in this

Preface xvii

study, Blau speaks to the importance of involving poor and homeless people in all coalitions advocating for more humane policies.

In conclusion, there is much that has been written about homelessness generally and homeless women in particular in the two years since I conducted this study. In reviewing this recent literature I often came up against my ongoing dilemma of activist versus scholar. Certainly enough studies have been done and enough has been written for us to break down stereotypes and create more humane social policies. But in reality I know it is a long hard journey. In this time of recession and budget deficits, there is not much hope for generous social welfare programs. While universal health care seems much more likely than it did a few years ago, there is still great resistance to higher, more progressive taxation. And still there is much ignorance about who these people are who do not have permanent homes--who live in shelters and on the streets. And thus, this study remains valuable as it gives voice to one small group of homeless individuals--middle-aged women without dependent children. There is much to be learned from their stories.

Sandy Butler
July, 1993

ACKNOWLEDGMENTS

In preparing this dissertation for publication I am deeply grateful for the patience and skill of Phoebe Nylund, Administrative Assistant at the School of Social Work at the University of Maine.

I would like to acknowledge each of the members of my dissertation committee from the Social Welfare Doctoral Program at the University of Washington in Seattle for their unique contributions. I am indebted to my Supervisory Chair, Dick Weatherley, for his friendship, his sense of humor, his political analysis, his assistance in developing this study, and for the frequent consultation over electronic mail while he was in Australia. Naomi Gottlieb, my Reading Chair, was the feminist mentor that every feminist scholar hopes for. Her belief in me, and in the value of having the stories of these women told, carried me through this project from start to finish. I am appreciative of Mary Gillmore's high standards, analytical thinking, and challenging questions. I thank Lew Gilchrist for her enthusiasm and her seemingly endless supply of research ideas. I am grateful to Christine Di Stephano, the Graduate Faculty Representative, for her feminist and Marxist analyses and for her encouragement to me as I struggled with my questions about the value of research on oppressed populations.

There were many friends that were important to me as I lived in two worlds--the world of homeless women and my academic world. I am appreciative of my colleagues, Lynne Dodson, Tracy Harachi and Jani Semke, with whom I shared many cups of coffee. Lynn Keenan, Linnea Flynn GlennMae, and Anne Nicoll provided timely and loving support by helping me over one obstacle or another in my doctoral adventure. Of all my friends, two stand out as being particularly helpful: Naomi Almeleh and Sue Steiner. Regular meetings with Naomi, her socialist-feminist analysis of my queries, and her support of me and my research, have turned what might have been a very isolating project into a collaborative one. Sue Steiner, my partner at the time, provided an invaluable combination of intellectual and emotional support throughout the data collection and dissertation writing. And finally I thank my parents who have been life-long friends, for being my initial and ever-lasting inspiration to work for social justice.

I wish to thank the service providers for their generosity and openness in sharing their time and their ideas. Most of all I thank the eleven women who shared their lives with me for six months.

INTRODUCTION

> Homelessness has in recent years captured the attention of the American public. Perhaps it is more accurate to say that homelessness has intruded itself upon the public consciousness. (Bachrach, 1987)

Homelessness is not a new social condition in this country, but the size and composition of the homeless population has changed so dramatically over the past two decades that it has become a condition that is increasingly difficult to ignore. Until recently, there has been little public sympathy for those who "chose" to be homeless; the homeless population was thought to consist primarily of middle-aged, alcoholic men, and people, (generally men), who chose a vagabond way of life. The smaller size of the homeless population, and the fact that the homeless were more likely to be confined to the "skid rows" of large cities, allowed homelessness to remain fairly invisible. The public conception that the homeless population was made up of irresponsible alcoholic "bums" served to keep this group among the ranks of the "undeserving poor"--i.e. those people undeserving of public aid. The changes in the numbers, visibility and composition of the homeless population, which have occurred in the past twenty years, have worked to alter public opinion about this phenomenon: is now considered a social problem.

Counting the homeless is nearly impossible. First, the definition of homelessness varies, and second, the methodological problems of counting people without a fixed residence are formidable. Baxter and Hopper (1981) urge caution in interpreting estimates:

> Any attempt to gauge the actual number of homeless people in a given area is subject to myriad difficulties. The estimates that do surface from time to time are notoriously unreliable, subject to wild discrepancies depending upon the methods of

estimation used, the source of the figures, the time of the year, and we strongly suspect, the purpose for which the numbers are put forth. The kinds of living arrangements defined as "homeless" may also vary considerably, adding a further element of uncertainty, and making historical and cross regional comparisons hazardous. (p.8)

Despite these difficulties, estimates of the number of homeless people abound--though the range is wide. The U.S. Department of Housing and Urban Development (HUD) comes in on the low side of estimated numbers of homeless individuals, with an estimate of 200,000 to 300,000, while advocates for the homeless estimate the number to be over two million. The U.S. Conference of Mayors conducted surveys twice in the past decade on the rate of homelessness in 25 representative cities. Most cities reported increases of 15 to 50 percent, and no city reported the numbers to be decreasing. While exact numbers cannot be known, both government officials and advocates for the homeless agree that the rate of homelessness is increasing (Institute of Medicine, 1988).

The National Alliance to End Homelessness emphasizes the fact that homelessness is not static. They estimate that on any given night in 1988 there were 735,000 homeless people in the U.S., but that throughout that year 1.3 to 2 million people were homeless for one or more nights (Institute of Medicine, 1988). But perhaps the 1988 estimate which is of most importance is that there were 6 million Americans who were constantly at risk of homelessness because of the disproportional amount of income poor people need to put into housing (Institute of Medicine, 1988).

The increase in homelessness in this country is the result of several political and economic factors. First, the diminishing availability of affordable housing is perhaps the most obvious reason for the growing numbers of homeless people. Since 1980, severe cuts in the federal budget have reduced government spending for affordable housing tremendously (Dreier & Atlas, 1989).

Secondly, compounding the problem of lack of low-cost housing, there have been many economic forces at work over the past two decades which have brought about an expansion of the lower class, and thus an increase in homelessness. Hopper and Hamberg (1984) summarize the trends--that began in the 1970's and were intensified in

Introduction xxiii

the 1980's--which have increased the ranks of the impoverished in this country:
1. Changing occupational composition of the U.S. labor force, resulting in many middle-income jobs being replaced by low-income jobs;
2. High divorce rate and the growth of female headed households which are more likely to be impoverished than male-headed households;
3. High levels of unemployment with reductions in Unemployment Insurance programs; and
4. Erosion of the real value of benefits in means-tested income maintenance programs, leaving recipients even less able to afford basic necessities than they were 15 years ago.

These economic trends have left an increasing number of families and individuals with incomes too low to afford both housing and basic necessities. Hopper and Hamberg (1984) estimate that one third of the nation's population are in this "shelter-poor" situation.

This research project is an attempt to understand better what the needs are of older, homeless women. There is great diversity among the homeless population, so no one set of services or programs will ever meet the needs of all the subgroups. Because older, single men have made up the largest proportion of the homeless population for many years, programs and services have been set up to meet their needs. It is reasonable to believe that these programs do not meet the needs of other subgroups in the homeless population. For example: young men may need job training and employment services; women with children may need services around domestic violence; older women may prefer shelter space that puts an emphasis on personal safety.

Homeless women now make up about 25 percent of the homeless populations, a jump from 3 percent in the early 1960's (Institute of Medicine, 1988). While public concern about vulnerable children without homes has led to increased research on the needs of homeless families and a growth in services particularly for them, homeless adult women without children have received far less attention.

What is known about homeless women comes primarily from anecdotal news stories or cross-sectional surveys seeking basic demographic statistics. There are many unanswered questions. For example: Little is known about how homeless women actually utilize programs and services, nor about what their perceptions are of these services. Since most research has been cross-sectional, there is a gap in our knowledge as to how women survive one day to the next, and how they cope with their homeless status. For this reason, a qualitative research approach was chosen for this study in order to understand from the homeless women's perspectives about their daily lives and service needs.

The subgroup of single adult homeless women can be divided further by age. As in the general population, one would expect that the issues for younger women would be different from those of middle-aged and elderly homeless women. Impoverished, middle-aged women make up a population which has received little attention from the media or academic community. Homeless, middle-aged women represent perhaps the most destitute portion of this understudied population. Middle-aged women without husbands or children--"unrelated individuals", as they are called in the census reports--have the very high rate of poverty of 25 percent (U.S. Bureau of the Census, 1991). Given this high rate of poverty, it is perhaps not surprising that the rate of homelessness among middle-aged women is rising as well. In order to understand the special needs of older, homeless women, the population focus of this study was homeless women aged 45 and older.

Seattle, Washington served as the site of this study. As a major harbor city with temperate weather, Seattle has always had its share of transients. But, similar to other areas of the country, Seattle has seen both a large increase in the number of homeless individuals, and a change in the composition of the homeless population, over the past two decades (Human Services Strategic Planning Office, 1989). Currently, conservative estimates of Seattle's homeless population range between 12,000 to 14,000 individuals each year; 2,000 to 2,500 people are without shelter on any given night in Seattle (Human Services Strategic Planning Office, 1989).

Service providers and city officials have noted an increase in the number of adult homeless women in the Seattle area over the past few years. They have expressed an interest in knowing more about homeless, middle-aged women--a group of people who, traditionally have kept to themselves, and whose responses to programs and services are far from predictable. Programs and housing options specifically for this population are needed and are being planned. Research focusing on

Introduction xxv

adult homeless women without children--particularly middle-aged women--is therefore important in the development of these programs.

FORMAT OF BOOK

Chapter 1 provides a review of the literature that informed this study. The research questions and the study methodology are presented in chapter 2. Chapter 3 provides a description of the sample and introduces the findings that are reported in Chapters 4 through 7. Using four themes from the data as a framework, the homeless women's past, present and future plans are presented in the first three chapters of the research findings: Chapter 4 discusses the women's pathways to homelessness; day to day lives are described in Chapter 5; and Chapter 6 presents the women's plans and hopes for the future. Chapter 7 discusses service needs for this population as viewed by the homeless women and by service providers. The concluding chapter provides a discussion of the findings and the policy implications of this study.

CHAPTER ONE

LITERATURE REVIEW

HOMELESSNESS: GENERAL OVERVIEW

In this section I begin by reviewing some of the general literature on homelessness, before examining what has been written specifically about homeless women. The topics I cover in this first part of the review, while applying to homelessness in general, provide a perspective for understanding some of the specific issues for homeless women. Topics are: 1) causes of homelessness, including: economic conditions, loss of low-income housing, deinstitutionalization, inadequate facilities for drug and alcohol treatment, and domestic violence; 2) services to the homeless; and 3) public responses to the homeless.

Causes of Homelessness

The homeless population of the U.S. is heterogeneous, and the antecedents to homelessness are necessarily complex. Nevertheless there are several broad social, political and economic factors which are generally considered to be responsible for the recent increase in homelessness: economic conditions, loss of low-income housing, deinstitutionalization of the mentally ill, inadequate facilities for drug and alcohol treatment, and inadequate supports for victims of domestic violence (Baxter & Hopper, 1981; Bachrach, 1987; Institute of Medicine, 1988; Roberts & Keefe, 1986; Wright, 1988).

Economic conditions. Between 1970 and 1980 the nonfarm sector of the United States experienced a decline in real wages of 7.4 percent. The median household income was the same at the end of the decade as it had been at the beginning only because more households had more than one wage earner in order to compensate for the decline in wages (Hopper & Hamberg, 1984). A significant and growing polarization of income distribution occurred during this time: the upper and particularly lower classes expanded while the middle class began to shrink (Hopper & Hamberg, 1984). Current data show that the economic gap between upper- and lower-income American families was wider in 1987 than at any time since the Census Bureau began collecting these data in 1947 (Karger & Stoesz, 1990). In 1977, the average family, in the richest one percent of American families, had an annual income of $301,000, (calculated in 1988 dollars); in 1988 that group averaged $452,000 per year (McIntyre, 1986). Furthermore, wealth became increasingly concentrated. By 1983 the top 0.5% of U.S. households owned 45 percent of all wealth--excluding personal residences--up 38 percent from 20 years earlier (Marcuse, 1983).

Unemployment is one major factor contributing to the rise of the "new poor" in the 1980's. Unemployment in the early 80's had some particular characteristics that account for some of the increase in homelessness during that decade. First, with the closing of an increasing number of manufacturing plants, many more of the unemployed in the recession of the early 80's experienced permanent job loss than did the unemployed in the recessions of the decade before--53.1 percent as opposed to 36 percent (Hopper & Hamberg, 1984). Secondly, those unemployed were more likely to stay jobless longer in the 80's than they were in the 70's. Twenty-five percent of all unemployed fell into the category of "long-term unemployed" having been out of work for six months or longer and therefore ineligible for Unemployment Insurance (UI) payments under 1981 legislation restricting "extended" benefits (Hopper & Hamberg, 1984).

In 1975, the unemployment rate was calculated at 8.5 percent and over 75 percent of the unemployed were covered by UI. In 1985, the unemployment rate had fallen to 7.2 percent, but only 33 percent were covered under the UI programs (Karger & Stoesz, 1990). In 1976, 1.9 million unemployed workers were not receiving unemployment benefits, by 1985 5.6 million unemployed workers were uninsured (Center on Budget and Policy Studies, 1985).

Literature Review

Reported unemployment rates do not tell the whole story as they exclude discouraged workers who are no longer seeking work as well as those who have returned to lower paying jobs and often part-time jobs (Karger & Stoesz, 1990). This was the situation in the 1980's when unemployment rates alone could not explain the rise in poverty and homelessness. Katz (1989) considers homeless individuals to be "casualties of the postindustrial city" (p.188). Many higher paying jobs have been removed from the cities with the exit of manufacturing, and the new jobs within the service sector, for which the homeless might qualify, pay wages that are too low to meet escalating housing costs (Katz, 1989).

Marcuse (1983) describes the link between homelessness and labor market conditions as follows:

> The structure of production is ultimately at the root of what happens in the housing market and of government policy. The influence is not always direct; it may in some cases not be decisive, but it is always present. The logic is straight forward: what the homeless get depends on how useful they are to the system, and how they deal with their position in it. When there is a shortage of labor, the poor are needed. Their housing is a concern, and very few end up homeless, as was the situation during World War II, and during the postwar boom. (p.130)

He asserts that it is not just unemployment that has led to the increase in homelessness, because the steady rise in the rate of homelessness has not been accompanied by a parallel rise in unemployment. Rather, it is the change in both the extent of employment and unemployment, and the power relationships of employers and employees. The decrease in manufacturing jobs and the rise in service sector jobs have been accompanied by these different power relations:

> Nothing inherent in the service sector dictates that its wages must be lower than those of the manufacturing sector. The fact that 44 percent of all new jobs created since 1980 pay poverty level wages has as much to do with the relationship between employers and workers as with the type of work involved. The type of work may facilitate an aggrandizement of power by an

employer, and may weaken the ability of a worker to insist on a decent wage, but it is ultimately conflict between the two that will decide how much is paid. (p. 130)

According to Marcuse's analysis, when the poor are militant and the establishment is concerned about their possible actions, the homeless cannot be rejected or isolated. But when labor is surplus, and the poor are quiescent, as is the case currently, then the poor are not served and homelessness increases (Marcuse, 1983). This analysis is not unlike that which is presented by Piven and Cloward (1971) in their seminal book *Regulating the Poor*. Piven and Cloward demonstrate how welfare benefits contract when the labor supply is in surplus, and expand when there is a shortage of labor, and when there is more potential of revolt from the labor class.

The plight of the poor also was worsened through cuts in public welfare programs in the early 1980's. From 1980 to 1984 means-tested programs in the federal budget were reduced 16.4 percent despite the increase in poverty (Ridgeway, 1984). As a result of 1981 regulations, which lowered the income level at which a family could be eligible for Aid to Families with Dependent Children (AFDC), 50 percent of the working families receiving AFDC lost eligibility; another 40 percent had their benefits reduced. Relief provided by state governments in the form of General Assistance (GA) dropped about 32 percent between 1970 and 1985, and aid for the disabled was severely restricted (Katz, 1989). The federal financial commitment to the disabled was also reduced dramatically.

In the early 1980's, the Reagan administration, as part of its war on welfare, successfully excised about 200,000 thousand disabled people, many with psychiatric disorders, from the roles of Supplemental Social Security. (Katz, 1989, p.189)

Studies of those whose benefits were terminated show that most often the loss of benefits were due to the impaired ability of the recipient to challenge the ruling, and not to a legitimate weeding from the ranks of those who had recovered their health. The mentally disabled were overrepresented among those who were terminated by a factor of three to one (Hopper & Hamberg, 1984).

Literature Review

Low-income housing availability. Poverty coupled with the nation-wide phenomenon of reduced availability of low-cost housing has resulted in the expanding numbers of homeless families and individuals. We are currently facing the most severe housing crisis since the 1930's. During the 1980's federal housing programs were cut by 80 percent--this was the largest cutback of any domestic program in the Reagan administration. Federal spending was reduced from over $33 billion to less than $8 billion (Dreier & Atlas, 1989).

Since 1980 the aggregate supply of low-income housing has declined by approximately 2.5 million units (Institute of Medicine, 1988). Each year it is estimated that approximately half a million low-cost housing units are lost through conversion, abandonment, fire, or demolition; the production of new housing has not kept pace (Institute of Medicine, 1988). Low-income people need to devote a much larger percentage of their income to housing than do people at higher income levels (Scott, 1984) and thus are at even greater risk of losing their housing through the inevitable unexpected crises that accompany poverty.

Housing starts barely kept pace with the increase in households in the early 80's, not to mention replacing units lost from inventory (Hopper & Hamberg, 1984). High interest rates placed a new or existing home out of the reach of many likely home buyers. In 1983, only 30 percent of "typical" home buyers--a married couple under 35 with 2 children--could afford to purchase a mid-priced house. In previous decades 65 percent could do so. The proportion of the population owning homes declined for the first time since the Depression (Hopper & Hamberg, 1984). Because so many would-be homeowners have become reluctant renters over the past decade, demand for apartments has increased dramatically (Dreier & Atlas, 1989).

Doubling up has been one consequence of this housing crisis. The number of families living with others as "subfamilies" doubled, from a low of 1.3 million in 1978, to 2.6 million in 1983; and the number of unrelated individuals living with others went from 23.4 million to 28.1 million in that same time period (Hopper & Hamberg, 1984). In New York City, 17,000 families were doubling up in public housing projects in the early 1980's--this doubling up affects one out of every ten households officially living in such projects (Hopper & Hamberg, 1984). There is an 18 year waiting list for public housing in New York

City, 20 years in Miami, and 12 years in Boston (Kozol, 1988). The U.S. Department of Housing and Urban Development (HUD) subsidies are only enough for 4.3 million households, about one-third of the need (The Women and Poverty Project, 1989).

In 1970, there were almost 15 million housing units that could be rented for the equivalent of 30 percent of a $5000 annual income. By 1985 there were only 1.8 million units, which is only about one unit for every two low-income households (The Women and Poverty Project, 1989). During the last decade, landlords have taken advantage of the tight rental market by raising rents and evicting tenants who fall behind in their rent payments. In New York City, with a total of 2 million rental units, steps were taken to evict nearly half a million households in 1983 (Hopper & Hamberg, 1984).

Hartman (1983) enumerates the goals behind the Reagan administration's reversal of the federal government's fifty-year-old commitment to provide housing aid for those that the market could not adequately serve. These goals were:

1. To virtually end all programs that directly add, through construction and substantial rehabilitation, to the stock of housing available to lower income households.
2. To reduce housing subsidy requirements by forcing recipients to devote higher proportions of their inadequate incomes to housing.
3. To reduce the existing stock of subsidized housing, through demolition, conversion, sale, and planned deterioration.
4. To rely exclusively on the existing housing supply to meet low-income housing needs. (Hartman, 1983, p.1-2)

The reductions of budgetary allocations that directly added to the available stock of low and moderate-income housing, the decline in quality and the sell-off of some public housing units, and the erosion of rent subsidies all meant that the poor began paying increasing portions of their incomes for an increasingly scarce commodity (Hopper & Hamberg, 1984).

It took Congress six years to react to the Reagan administration's housing goals.

> Housing was only a marginal issue when President Reagan was elected in 1980. His administration carried out the

recommendations of the 1981 President's Housing Task Force, which called for the virtual elimination of federal housing assistance and greater reliance on the private market system. For the first six years Congress put up little resistance and allowed housing to shoulder the largest chunk of the Reagan budget axe. (Dreier & Atlas, 1989, p.30)

By 1987 the housing question appeared back on the political agenda in Congress, and Senator Alan Cranston, chair of the Senate Housing Subcommittee, put out word that he was looking for new ideas for a comprehensive housing policy for the 1990's (Dreier & Atlas, 1989). Many housing bills have been filed since then. According to Dreier and Atlas (1989), these bills do not provide the commitment to housing that is needed to meet our current housing crisis.

The housing crisis has not yet become politically volatile enough to force Congress or HUD to act dramatically--to shift Pentagon resources into housing, to increase taxes on the wealthy and big business, or to call for a universal entitlement to decent housing. (p.31)

Deinstitutionalization of the mentally ill. The actual percentage of mentally ill individuals among the homeless is unknown. It is thought that while alcoholism is more widespread among homeless men, severe psychopathology may be more common among homeless women (Bachrach, 1985; Stark, 1986; Bassuk, Rubin & Lauriet, 1984). "Deinstitutionalization" is often blamed for the increase in homelessness.

Broadly defined, deinstitutionalization includes more than the mere release of patients from state mental hospitals. It also encompasses a civil libertarian philosophy that is manifested in preclusive commitment procedures in many states. Accordingly, chronically mentally ill individuals are often caught in an ideological Catch-22 situation, and their needs for adequate treatment and assured housing are subordinated to their right to live "freely" in "nonrestrictive" settings. (Bachrach, 1987, p. 380)

Although the philosophy behind deinstitutionalization may have been well-intended, with the patients' rights in mind, the consequences, due to inadequate community-based substitutes, have been devastating for thousands of individuals.

In most instances the route from hospital to homelessness has been a circuitous one. The vast majority of patients were placed in housing on release from hospitals, but often in arrangements that were easily disrupted for individuals not used to managing on their own. The other side of deinstitutionalization is the tightened admitting criteria in most psychiatric facilities. Many individuals who formerly would have been hospitalized are now turned away. As the number of residential hotels, or single room occupancy hotels (SRO's), has declined, even housing of last resort has been hard to find (Hopper and Hamberg, 1984).

Substance abuse and domestic violence. Though there is some evidence that substance abuse is less prevalent among adult homeless women than among homeless men (Bachrach, 1987; Gilchrist, 1990; Multnomah County, 1985), it remains a debilitating problem for a high proportion of both sexes (Institute of Medicine, 1988; Corrigan & Anderson, 1984; Garret & Bahr, 1976; Multnomah County, 1985, 1984; Baxter & Hopper, 1981). Lack of adequate treatment facilities, and after care housing, adds thousands of individuals to the ranks of the homeless.

Finally, one cause of homelessness for single women and female-headed families is physical violence by a partner or spouse (Multnomah County, 1985; Slavinsky & Cousins, 1982; Stoner, 1983). Though shelters for battered women and their families are much more available than they were 20 years ago, they are always time-limited, and women who choose not to return to the battering situation may not have the financial means to set up independent living.

Services to the Homeless

There has not been a great deal of literature on how well available services meet the needs of homeless individuals. Baxter and Hopper (1981) examined the lives of the homeless in New York City and the shelters available to them. *Private Lives/Public Lives* is their much respected and quoted report on the deficiencies in the social service and shelter network set up in the New York City area. Three of their major findings were: 1) people do not "choose" to live on the street when there is decent, humane shelter available; 2) owing to restrictive intake procedures and dangerous, degrading conditions, public shelter has definite deterrent features intrinsic to it; and 3) life on the streets is a complex feat of survival--a demeaning, full-time occupation demanding resourcefulness, courage and great endurance.

Hopper, Baxter, Cox and Klein (1982) followed up this report with a second, fact finding project on progress made over a year's period. They found remarkable improvement in one year's time, though distressing deficiencies remained in available shelter and other services to the homeless. Some of the changes they documented were: 1. the Callahan suit was settled--a decree which committed the city to provide clean and safe shelter for every man and woman who sought it (Katz, 1989); 2. the public shelter system in New York City had expanded considerably; 3. there was an increase in the number of homeless people availing themselves of shelters and drop-in centers; 4. mental health authorities had made progress in endorsing the notion that special facilities were needed to house the proportion of the homeless with psychiatric disabilities; 5. the media was better informed and more sympathetic with respect to homelessness; 6. the public seemed better disposed toward the homeless, including a public consensus that at least the homeless deserve shelter; and 7. numerous groups emerged to serve as vocal advocates for the homeless.

The American Psychiatric Association (APA) (Levine & Rog, 1990) conducted interdisciplinary site visits to programs across the country that serve homeless mentally ill persons. Some of their major findings were:

1. Approximately one third of the homeless population have severe mental illnesses such as schizophrenia and mood disorders.
2. The homeless mentally ill population is a multi-need population; in some studies, as much as 50 percent of homeless, mentally ill individuals also have a substance abuse problem.
3. A sizeable number of homeless mentally ill people have had involvements with the criminal justice system.
4. Many homeless mentally ill persons have never received mental health treatment, and many homeless individuals,

formerly in treatment, are no longer disabled by mental illness.
5. Homeless mentally ill individuals tend to place a priority on meeting their basic subsistence needs first, before addressing their mental health needs, whereas mental health professionals may place a higher priority on providing traditional mental health treatment (Levine & Rog, 1990).

In 1985 and 1987, the National Institute of Mental Health, (NIMH), Community Support Program provided funding support for 20 small-scale pilot demonstration projects focused on developing services for homeless mentally ill adults.

> Evidence from these projects suggests that discrete service elements cannot address the multiple, diverse, and extensive needs of the homeless mentally ill population. For example, case management services are dependent upon the ability of case managers to refer their clients to available housing, treatment and other community resources. Thus the experiences of these projects, as well as the findings of NIMH-sponsored research, suggest the need for a more comprehensive approach to service delivery. (Levine & Rog, 1990, pp.964-5)

The Stewart B. McKinney Homeless Assistance Act (Public Law 100-77, 1987) provides the first federal funds targeted specifically to address the health, education and welfare needs of the homeless population. The Act authorized funds for demonstration programs for homeless individuals who are chronically mentally ill. Services provided by these programs include: 1. outreach services in nontraditional settings, e.g. the street and drop-in centers; 2. intensive long-term case management; 3. mental health treatment including screening, diagnosing and medication management; 4. staffing and operation of supportive living programs; and 5. management and administrative activities designed to link together services (Levine & Rog, 1990). Block grants for these services are allocated to all states and territories on a formula weighted toward urbanized areas. An initial review of the funding applications for the first two years of funding show considerable diversity in the services provided (Levine & Rog, 1990).

Literature Review 11

Services to adult single women will be discussed in more detail later in this review, but homeless women with children are another group with special service needs. Diana Pearce (1988) calls women and children the invisible homeless. They have good reason to remain invisible because officials are obligated by law to make sure children are not without shelter and may place children in foster care if a woman with children applies for shelter and no shelter is available. Once the children are in foster care it is difficult to get them back. Pearce lists five ways in which homeless women with children remain invisible, thus not being counted in the statistics and not being adequately considered in the development of services: 1. they are more likely to double up with families and friends; 2. they seek hidden housing such as cars and abandoned buildings; 3. they may be homeless due to battering and thus go to shelters for battered women; 4. they may informally leave their children with relatives and friends; and 5. rather than expose their children to life in a shelter, they may voluntarily place their children into foster care. Recognizing the invisibility of this group is important in understanding the scope and nature of the problem and in formulating programs and policies to meet their needs.

Public Responses to the Homeless

Roberts and Keefe (1986) describe the country's response to homelessness as "sporadic and insufficient". These authors accurately describe as residual responses to homelessness efforts to provide temporary housing, food, aid in finding work, and assistance with day to day dilemmas. People who work with the homeless are aware how inadequate this type of response is for dealing with such a complex, persistent problem. Research on the gaps in service such a residual approach inevitably produces, would be beneficial for policy makers and advocates for the homeless, who are working toward broader and more humane solutions to this social problem.

Americans have always found it necessary to distinguish between the deserving and undeserving poor. Wright (1988) discusses how polls of public opinion on homelessness are mixed on this issue. He notes that a national survey by the Roper Organization found in 1987 that 68% of its respondents considered "caring for the homeless" to be a top priority. But Wright also quotes a more "mean-spirited" analysis of homelessness authored by Stuart Bykofsky which appeared in *Newsweek* in 1986.

> The analysis turned on the division of the homeless into three groups: "(1) the economically distressed who would work if they could find work; (2) the mentally ill who can't work; (3) the alcoholic, the drug-addicted, and others who won't work." His solution to the problems was workfare for the first group, mental institutions for the second, and indifference to (or outright hostility toward) the third. (p.64)

Former President Reagan, in a farewell interview with David Brinkley in December of 1988, made this comment on homelessness:

> They make it their own choice for staying out there...There are shelters in virtually every city, and shelters here, and those people still prefer out there on the grates or the lawn to going into one of those shelters. ("Reagan on Homelessness", 1988)

HOMELESS WOMEN/ FEMALE POVERTY AT MIDLIFE

In this section I present literature in two areas especially pertinent to this research: homeless women and impoverished women at mid-life. Exploratory research in the previously, little-studied, area of homeless women has significantly increased in the past decade, while poverty among women at mid-life remains an area that has received very little research attention.

Homeless Women

In the preface to the photograph/essay book by Rousseau, *Shopping Bag Ladies: Homeless Women Speak About Their Lives* (1981), Alix Kates Shulman discusses the lack of attention homeless women have received in the literature:

> Why have homeless women received so much less attention and care than homeless men? Principally of course, for the

> same reasons that women everywhere in our society have received relatively little public attention, whether from public servants, historians, employers, legislators, or shapers of consciousness: In a society in which women have little power, their lives are considered unimportant compared to the lives of men. (p.11)

Slavinsky and Cousins (1982) emphasize that myths about homeless women will prevail until more research focuses on who these women are, why they are on the street and why they behave as they do. Stoner (1983) claims that services to homeless women will suffer as long as their needs are not well understood:

> ... research is needed that does not treat women as derelicts but as homeless people with specific women's problems and needs. This is necessary because the apparent systematic avoidance of dealing with homeless women in research and literature suggests that women receive harsher judgement and less adequate services than men even at this marginal level of society. As women and their families continue to enter the ranks of the homeless--as victims of the economy, of landlords, of a depleted mental health system, and of spouses--society can no longer neglect them (p.568)

In the eight years since Stoner wrote the above statement, there has been a considerable increase in research on this population. Descriptive surveys on samples of homeless women in Portland, Oregon (Anderson, Boe & Smith, 1988), Albany, New York (Hagen & Ivanoff, 1988), and St. Louis, Missouri (Johnson & Kreuger, 1989), add to our knowledge about the life histories and general characteristics of individuals in this population.

Anderson, Boe and Smith (1988) surveyed 190 homeless women in Portland, Oregon. They found most of their respondents to be young, with minor children and to be mobile. The majority were in poor health and had a history of physical or sexual abuse. One quarter were alcoholic and 18 percent had had psychiatric treatment. The authors advocate a flexible treatment approach with a strong case management component to help homeless women resolve their problems and gain some control over their lives.

One strength of this study is that it provides new data on a relatively large sample of homeless women recruited from a variety of sites. The information collected from the 70-item questionnaire offers a cross-sectional view of the experience of homelessness for women in Portland, Oregon. One weakness of the study is that the one-time contact with the subjects, and a questionnaire with standardized questions and responses, placed some restrictions on the depth of the understanding the researchers could obtain from the women about how they experienced homelessness.

Hagen and Ivanoff (1988) interviewed 51 homeless women in Albany, New York. They found their sample to be a very heterogeneous group with diverse mental health and social service needs. Family stress, including intergenerational conflict, marital discord and domestic violence, was a key reason given for homelessness, though one half of the women maintained close ties with a variety of family members and friends. One third of the sample had experienced a psychiatric hospitalization and reported high levels of current mental health complaints. Forty percent reported substance abuse to be one of three reasons for their homelessness. Economic vulnerability characterized all the women. Employment was the major source of income for one quarter of the women, while most women depended on public assistance and help from family and friends. The authors recommend safe, affordable housing and transitional living environments with supportive services. They emphasize that a range of alternatives will be necessary given the heterogeneity of the population. Similar to Anderson et. al (1988), Hagen and Ivanoff obtained their data from structured questionnaires administered to the subjects in one-time interviews; the opportunity for the homeless women to share their stories may have been restricted by this format.

Johnson and Kreuger (1989) analyzed data on 240 women collected by Health Care for the Homeless in St. Louis, Missouri in order to examine differences between homeless women with and without children. They found that the homeless women without children in their sample were more likely to be older, white women "who exhibit higher levels of individual dysfunction than the generally younger minority women (black in the case of St. Louis) who compose female-headed households" (p.539). Women without children tended to have been homeless longer, were more likely to have been hospitalized for psychiatric problems, to have had recent contact with a mental

Literature Review

health professional, more likely to drink, and to have been told they had a drinking problem. The authors suggest their data provide preliminary support for using the presence or absence of dependent children as an initial indicator in developing a typology of homeless women, leading to differing programs for the two subgroups. They argue that homeless women without children need more intensive psychological services, including psychiatric counseling and alcohol treatment, while women with children may need more socioeconomic support.

Some research has been done on using group work with homeless women (Breton, 1988) and with homeless, mentally ill women (Berman-Rossi & Cohen, 1988) as a tool for empowerment.

Breton (1988) describes a nurturing/educating approach used by the Toronto drop-in center, Sistering, serving homeless women. The center attempts to offer not only a refuge for rest and recuperation, but also a program emphasizing competence. This is a difficult and delicate balance as described by the author:

> As Sistering tries to help these women to overcome the effects of their victimization, it faces the dilemma that in dealing with oppressed people, it is easy to try to compensate for their victimization in a paternalistic manner that creates further helplessness. It is easy to oppress the oppressed by seeing them as victims, and not as whole persons, thereby stigmatizing them instead of collaborating towards their empowerment. It must be acknowledged that the empowerment of oppressed people is a complex process. On the one hand, one must guard against false empowerment, or against pretending that environments can always be manipulated in one's favor. On the other hand, one cannot settle for less than doing whatever it is possible to do. (p.48)

The author suggests the use of small "mutual-aid" groups as an empowering tool with this population in order to meet both the nurturing and education goals of such agencies.

Berman-Rossi and Cohen (1989) describe the success of mental health workers organizing mentally ill women who were living in an SRO hotel into a "dinner group". This group increased the social and daily living skills of the participants, increased mutual aid, increased a sense of community, and increased participants' feeling of taking responsibility for themselves. "The cooking group provided structure around which severely emotionally disabled women were able to sustain themselves and each other and to experience some new level of competence" (p.75).

The National Institute of Mental Health advocates ethnographic research in order to better understand the unique needs of homeless women (Koegel, 1986). Some qualitative research does exist on this population. Rousseau (1981) describes the lives of "shopping bag" women through the format of photographs and the telling of their stories in their own words. Stark (1986) presents four case histories of chronically mentally ill homeless women depicting the importance of the sense of independence these women develop on the street, and the necessity for service programs to foster that trait. The author argues that the belief that chronically mentally ill, homeless individuals will not adjust to the structured environment of residential facilities does not hold up in the light of the fact that such individuals already lead very structured lives on the streets. They have developed skills in order to survive on the streets that are often much more demanding than those required to live in a residential facility.

> For this reason, residential facilities for the homeless chronically mentally ill must be based on the skills that their clients bring with them, and must be developed accordingly.... Rather than settle for simple caretaking and warehousing, they should build upon the sense of independence that their streetwise clients bring with them, seeing this as a strength that can perhaps lead to some sort of rehabilitation. (p. 110)

Hand (1983) and Martin (1982) both used ethnographic methods to study strategies of survival for homeless women in New York City. Hand (1983) observed 25 women she categorized as "shopping bag women" given their common characteristics of being homeless, disaffiliated, socially withdrawn, and living in urban public places. She discovered different personal styles or types of behavior exhibited by these women: the "lady", the "pretender", and the "beggar". Despite differences in style, all the women seemed to have a common adaptive goal: to take advantage of the free accessibility to goods, buildings, services and facilities offered by an affluent city. They tended to fit themselves into existing environments and participate in established routines rather than attempt to disrupt or displace other persons or ongoing activities.

Martin (1982) explored coping strategies of urban transient women. She identified two types of strategies: street survival strategies to meet basic needs and maintenance strategies that lessen the impact of stress. She suggests that service programs for homeless women should be developed to reflect not only an understanding of health, mental health and social welfare fields, but also an understanding of the lifestyles and adaptation techniques used by women who have been living on the street.

In an effort to understand the meaning of homelessness for homeless women, Merves (1986) gathered the life histories of 15 homeless women--with and without children--in Columbus, Ohio. The women reported experiencing either a precipitous slide into homelessness and poverty, or a critical event which caused them to be homeless. She found the women's value systems to be similar to those of the larger society: they wanted independence, self-sufficiency and success. Often they felt inadequate or embarrassed at not being able to live up to these values.

These recent qualitative studies have been important in dismantling myths about homeless women. Still more information is needed on how women cope from one day to the next, how they use services over a period of time, how their lives change over time, and how their beliefs and values affect their behaviors and choices (Koegel, 1986).

The above studies on homeless women do not always distinguish between those homeless women with children and those without. Johnson and Kreuger (1989) did make this distinction and investigated the differences between the two groups. Their data showed that on average women without children in their sample tended to be older, to have been homeless longer, to be more likely to have, or have history of having, psychiatric and/or substance abuse problems, than did the homeless women with children. This lends support to the notion that service needs may differ for single homeless women than for women who have children with them.

Impoverished Middle-Aged Women

Another understudied population of women is that of impoverished middle-aged women. (For purposes of this discussion, middle-aged will be defined as 45 to 64 years of age.) Although public awareness of the feminization of poverty has led to research about younger women heading families and frail elderly women--poor women at mid-life have been virtually ignored (Butler & Weatherley, 1992; Cahn, 1978; Kutza, 1978; Berlin & Jones, 1983). The high rate of poverty experienced by middle-aged women living without family, (discussed below), makes them particularly vulnerable to homelessness

There are many reasons why women may be vulnerable to poverty when they reach their middle years. Women who have been socialized to be homemakers and dependent on a spouse's income, may find themselves destitute at mid-life due to separation, divorce or widowhood (Lopata & Brehm, 1986; Sommers & Shields, 1978). AFDC mothers who have depended on public assistance while bringing up their children will find themselves without support once their youngest child reaches 18 (Berlin & Jones, 1983). There is a hole in the country's safety net through which poor middle-aged women without dependent children and without disabilities will fall (Block, Davidson & Grambs, 1981; Lopata & Brehm, 1986; Kutza, 1978).

Even women at mid-life who are able to work, may well find themselves in part-time, low-wage work without benefits, leaving them vulnerable to poverty (Nuccio, 1989; Bergmann, 1986). Caregiving responsibilities to dependent adults often fall to middle-aged women, making entry into full-time work more difficult (Brody, 1981; Hooyman, 1989; Gottlieb, 1989) Lack of skills, or what Kutza (1978) refers to as "functional disability", may keep many women from gaining any sort of employment, though they remain ineligible for any type of assistance. Additionally the bulk of the low-skill jobs created in the past two decades which would be available to these women have been in the service sector. Unlike the higher wage manufacturing jobs that used to be more available, these tend to be part-time, low-wage, and without benefits.

Among poor middle-aged women there is one group that stands out in the statistics on poverty due to a particularly high rate of poverty. "Unrelated middle-aged women"--that is women who are not living with partners, children, or other family members--had a rate of poverty of 25 percent in 1990. For middle-aged white women it was 22 percent and for middle-aged black women, 43 percent (U.S. Bureau of the Census, 1991). Compared to "unrelated middle-aged women", "unrelated" women 25 to 44 years of age experienced a much lower rate of poverty--about 15 percent. As women grew older, their rates of poverty increased in 1990 in this "unrelated" category: 25 percent for the 65 to 74 years of age range, and 28.7 percent for those women 75 and older (U.S. Bureau of the Census, 1991). This does not bode well for single women who are impoverished in middle-age and among all middle-aged women, it is this group of single women that may be most vulnerable to becoming homeless.

CONCLUSION

The stories of middle-aged impoverished women who are experiencing homelessness have not been adequately told. Like other subpopulations among the homeless they have been grouped together because of one common denominator--being without a home. The research questions which guided this study attempt to gain an understanding of the lives of single, middle-aged, homeless women; these questions have not been well addressed in the literature to date. Hearing in their own words about how they became homeless, what their lives are like as older women without homes, how they view the social services they do access, and what their plans and hopes are for the future, is important for a more complete understanding of the phenomenon of homelessness as it is experienced by this subgroup. Planning policies and programs that cater to the particular needs of older, single homeless women will depend on such an understanding.

CHAPTER 2

METHOD

INTRODUCTION

A qualitative study was chosen to answer the research questions posed by this study. The research goals are presented below followed by the overall methodological approach of the study. There were three parts to this study: interviewing homeless women, interviewing service providers, and observation at agencies. The primary focus of the study was the first of these: interviewing middle-aged homeless women and the focus of this chapter is on the methods and procedures used in learning about their lives. The methods used in interviewing service providers and in doing observation are discussed at the end of the chapter.

RESEARCH GOALS AND QUESTIONS

My research questions arose from the following four goals:
1. To learn about the pathways to homelessness for the women in my sample, how they perceive their current situation and future possibilities, and how they spend time on a day to day basis;
2. To understand, from a homeless woman's perspective, how existing social services, programs and housing options, as well as informal networks, meet and do not meet her needs, as she defines them, and how she utilizes these formal and informal networks on a day to day basis;
3. To learn how to stay in contact with such a transient population over a six month period of time; and

4. To learn, from service providers' perspectives, about how existing policies, programs and services for homeless women in the Seattle area meet and do not meet the needs of this population.

Questions under the first goal include:
1. In the subject's view, what brought her to her homeless situation?
2. What are her hopes, fears and concerns for the future?
3. How does she spend her time on a day to day basis?

Questions under the second goal include:
1. How does she use existing programs for the homeless? (e.g. What services does she use? How often? How did she learn about them? Which services does she avoid and why?)
2. What barriers does she perceive in accessing programs? What things make it easy for her to access programs?
3. Which programs work well for her? Which do not?
4. What would she like to see changed?
5. Does she feel she has rights? How does she exercise them?
6. Does she want permanent housing? If so, what kind? If not, why not?
7. What is the nature of her informal support network?

Questions under the third goal include:
1. Is it possible to stay in contact with homeless individuals over time?
2. What methods seem to be the most helpful in my efforts to stay in contact with women?
3. Could these methods be used in a larger scale study and what additional resources would be necessary?

Questions under the fourth goal include:
1. From the service provider's perspective, how well are existing programs meeting the needs of this population?
2. What gaps in services do they find most troubling?
3. Which programs have been most successful and why?
4. From the service provider's point of view, what barriers do homeless women confront in trying to access services?
5. What are the visions of service providers for better serving this population?

OVERALL METHODOLOGICAL APPROACH

Different research questions suggest different methodologies. One primary decision that a researcher must make is whether to use a quantitative or qualitative approach in order to answer a particular research question or set of questions, or both. The main intent of this research project was to understand about the lives of middle-aged, single, homeless women from the point of view of the women themselves. A qualitative research approach was chosen as the best method for entering into, and learning about, the women's lives.

Under the broad category "qualitative methods" there exist many theoretical perspectives and distinct methodologies. The methodology used in this study of homeless women drew on a variety sociological perspectives, while not being wedded to any particular one. Denzin (1978) describes the research method that involves actively entering into the worlds of interacting individuals as "naturalistic behaviorism". This method attempts to develop theories about interaction that rest on the behaviors, languages, definitions and attitudes of those studied. It draws on the perspective of symbolic interactionism:
Symbolic interactionism rests on three basic assumptions.

> First, social reality as it is sensed, known, and understood is a social production. Interacting individuals produce and define their own definitions of situations. Second, humans are assumed to be capable of engaging in "minded", self-reflexive behavior. They are capable of shaping and guiding their own behavior and that of others. Third, in the course of taking their own standpoint and fitting that standpoint to the behaviors of others, humans interact with one another. Interaction is seen as an emergent, negotiated, often unpredictable concern. Interaction is symbolic because it involves the manipulation of symbols, words, meanings, and languages. (Denzin, 1978, p.7)

Similarly, phenomenological research has as its guiding theme: returning back to the things themselves (Swanson-Kauffman & Schonwald, 1988). Imperative to this type of research is to turn to the people who actually live the experience in order to accurately interpret phenomena. Phenomenological researchers strive to understand and describe lived experiences (Swanson-Kauffman & Schonwald, 1988).

The grounded theory approach as described by Glaser and Strauss (1967) is also closely tied to symbolic interactionism (Strauss, 1987). This approach emphasizes discovering meaning and theory from a comparative analysis of the data. The "constant comparative method of qualitative analysis" described by these authors involves a joint collection and analysis of the data. Theory emerges from the data as the end result of the delineation of categories and patterns, comparing incidents applicable to each category, integrating categories and their properties, and finally delimiting theory (Glaser & Strauss, 1967).

As mentioned in the previous chapter, the National Institute of Mental Health (NIMH) calls for increased ethnographic research on homeless women. At a national NIMH colloquium for social scientists involved in research on homeless women, the following rationale was given for qualitative methods:

> The rampant heterogeneity of the homeless population points to the fact that efforts to help the homeless must at least in part be sensitive to the problems, experiences, needs, and values of the various groups which together comprise the homeless population...it is somewhat unfortunate that research efforts aimed at understanding contemporary homelessness have relied almost exclusively on cross-sectional designs featuring structured interviews with individuals at one point in time...data from sample surveys are not by themselves capable of revealing all we need to know about homeless individuals to fully understand and effectively provide services to them. They tell us little about how homeless individuals actually make it from one day to the next--the resources they draw upon to meet their needs, the kinds of crises they face, and their strategies for solving them. They tell us little about the oscillations in their circumstances and the changing nature of their adaptation over time. Yet further, they tell us little about how homeless individuals themselves perceive their experiences, and how their beliefs and values affect their behavior, choices, and willingness to accept certain kinds of services. They tell us little, in other words, about those areas which have traditionally fallen within the purview of more

qualitative approaches to the study of human behavior. (Koegel, 1986, pp.2-3)

Three additional reasons for using ethnographic methodologies in studying homeless women, in particular, were emphasized by colloquium participants: 1) to better understand gender-related issues; 2) to undermine the myths that persist about homeless women; 3) to model a trusting relationship--that between researcher and participant--that can be used in worker-client interactions (Koegel, 1986).

Swanson-Kauffman (1986) struggles with choosing the right qualitative research methodology in doing nursing research. Her concerns for research in the nursing profession reflect my own confusion in choosing the correct methodology for a study exploring questions about social welfare:

Nurses must explore how best to study their own concerns. We need to allow ourselves the comfort to recognize that those values and methods that hold up well elsewhere should not dictate how we choose to go about answering questions that arise from our science or humanistic practice. A science of humans will seek to generate those methods that allow us to study and value persons as holistic, unique individuals who are in the process of becoming and who must be studied in their own environment. Simply put, we should let our nursing questions guide our methods while being ever aware that the methods will shape our answers. (pp.59-60)

In her study on the human experience of miscarriage and the caring need of women who miscarry, Swanson-Kauffman settles on a "unique blend of phenomenological, grounded theory, and ethnographic methodologies" (p.59) to guide her research. My own research on the experience of homelessness for middle-aged, single women, and on the policies and programs that might best meet their needs was also guided by a blend of the qualitative methodologies and perspectives discussed above.

INTERVIEWS WITH HOMELESS WOMEN

Sample Selection and Shelter Description

Criteria for being in sample. Purposive sampling (Miles & Huberman, 1984)--similar to selective sampling (Schatzman & Strauss, 1973))--was used to secure a sample of older, single homeless women. This type of sampling involves making decisions in advance to sample certain places and people. Before starting sample recruitment, I had calculated that I would be able to stay in contact with about twelve women because I would be trying to see each woman every other week. My final sample was composed of eleven women. My intention was to have at least four women of color in my sample as approximately one-third of the homeless female population in the area are women of color. My final sample had three women of color.

In order to be eligible for the study the women had to be 45 or older and without a permanent place of residence at the time of recruitment. Although participants could have had children living with them in the past, in order to be in the sample they needed to be living without children at the time of recruitment. Women with or without history of, or current experience with, substance abuse, mental illness or battering were eligible to be in the study. My original plan had been to interview only women who were considered chronically homeless in that they had been without a home for greater than 50 percent of preceding year. Given the difficulty I experienced in recruitment, and the sensitivity of asking such a question in an initial meeting, I dropped the criterion of chronic homelessness in the first weeks of recruitment.

Selecting shelters. Two shelters which serve homeless women in the Seattle area served as my initial source of participants for the study. These shelters--Downtown Emergency Services Center (DESC) and the Lutheran Compass Center (LCC)--will be described below. Although many shelters in Seattle serve homeless women with and without children, these were the two shelters which service providers suggested I access when I started data collection--they were known to be the shelters most often used by single homeless women. Children are not allowed at either of these shelters. DESC and LCC have very different programs and thus appeal to different subsets within the population of single homeless women. The first eight women in my sample came from these two shelters.

One month into data collection I posted flyers about my study at DESC and LCC and also in a day drop-in center for single homeless women, Angeline's (described below). Two women in my sample responded to flyers that they saw at Angeline's; one of these women was staying at DESC at the time of our first meeting and the other woman was staying at a shelter serving both families and single women. Three months into recruitment a temporary, emergency shelter was set up for single homeless women during the winter months. The last woman in my sample came from this shelter--the Women's Shelter (described below); I believe she first learned about the study from a flyer posted at Angeline's.

The descriptions of the three shelters and drop-in center which I provide below were true as of spring 1991. I have no doubt there have been changes in all four programs since that time.

Downtown Emergency Services Center. This agency was primarily a men's shelter. It was open 24 hours a day, 12 months of the year. Facilities were basic: men slept on the floor on mats and the atmosphere was crowded and noisy. Between 220 and 230 adults slept there each night. Women were never turned away from this shelter-- though men often were when the agency was filled to capacity--and staff have noted an increase in the number of women over the preceding two years. Between 40 and 60 women stayed at DESC each night. Women slept in a roped off section on bunk beds. Some of the women using this shelter were situationally homeless, while others had "lived" at DESC for years.

Lutheran Compass Center. This was a fairly structured program for adult homeless women. There were 16 beds spread out among private and semi-private rooms. Women could stay up to two months at LCC. One goal of the program was to help women get into more permanent settings after completing the program. Some women left before their two months were up without letting staff know where they were going. Women could return to the program after a period away. LCC served both situationally and chronically homeless women.

Angeline's. This was a day drop-in center for homeless women. Women can come and go as they pleased here with no restrictions placed on them. It was open Monday through Saturday and provided coffee, a telephone, showers, a place to be safe, a place to talk to other homeless women or service providers, or a place to be quiet. Women who were no longer homeless often continued to use Angeline's services.

Winter Women's Shelter. This shelter opened on December 10, 1990 and was originally scheduled to close on March 31, 1991, but it was granted a two month extension as plans were being made for an alternative shelter space for women. In response to collective action by homeless individuals in the form of a tent city, the city of Seattle opened two additional shelters during the winter months.

Other than LCC, which was relatively small and always full, the Women's Shelter was the first shelter in Seattle serving only adult homeless women. Its hours were from 5:30 pm to 7 am every day. Fifty women could be accommodated on mats on the floor; the shelter stayed full throughout the winter months. Women could return nightly for any length of time, and similar to DESC there were no expectations in terms of meeting goals or doing chores. Several of the women in my sample who had been staying at DESC at the beginning of my study eventually moved to the Women's Shelter, as they became aware of its existence and felt comfortable in making such a change in their lives.

Recruitment

I came in contact with the women in my study in different ways. Two participants were referred to me by LCC. Recruitment from this small shelter program with much staff-resident interaction worked best by having staff approach residents they knew to be 45 years of age or older in order to explain my study to them. Interested residents then contacted me by phone and we set up the first interview.

Six participants learned of my study while staying at DESC. Because of the size of this shelter, and the loose structure, one staff person helped me to organize an informational meeting for older female residents at the beginning of my data collection period. I sent letters to all the female residents over the age of 45 staying at the shelter on one night in mid-September--18 letters were sent. (Many homeless people receive mail at DESC.) Three women came to this meeting; I don't think that they came because of having received the letter, but rather because at the time of the meeting my staff liaison went around and personally invited women to come. All three of these women became a part of my sample; we set up our first interviews at the end of the meeting. The other three women recruited from DESC contacted me by phone after seeing my flyer posted at the shelter, or hearing about me from other residents or staff.

The final three women in my sample learned of my study at Angeline's, the day, drop-in center. They either called me directly after seeing the flyer or contacted a staff person at Angeline's for more information before calling.

In explaining the study to potential participants I let them know that I would pay them $5 each time we met, and that we could meet at restaurants or coffee shops where I would buy them coffee, a snack, a meal, or whatever they wanted.

Staying in Contact with my Sample

A methodological goal of this pilot study--goal number three mentioned above--was to learn how to stay in contact with a transient population over a six month period of time. I was quite successful in maintaining contact with my sample and will describe in this section some of the techniques that I used.

The primary technique was a combinations of persistence, tenacity and the will not to give up. At LCC I would leave phone messages for women which they would get if they were still living there; because of rules about confidentiality, staff could not inform me if women were still at the shelter. At DESC there is a large bulletin board where residents can receive messages organized by the days of the week. A note can stay on the board for seven days. I used this board regularly and received messages on it myself. Four of the women secured some sort of housing during the six month period; three of these women eventually had their own phones or a community phone at which I could leave messages. I sent letters to three of these women when they did not have phones. One woman had a post office box in a northern suburb which she checked periodically and I sent her letters there. Four women had intermittent employment; I would try to reach them at their work place as a last resort. All three of these methods: notes at shelters, letters in the mail, and phone calls worked well in maintaining contact with participants.

At the end of each interview, the participant and I would set up our next meeting which I would write down on a piece of paper for her along with my phone number. Early on in data collection I decided to give participants my home phone number so as to be sure to get all their phone calls. (There had been some confusion with receiving messages at the School of Social Work.) This also promoted an added element of trust to the relationships I was developing with the women. The five dollar payments, and the meals that I purchased for them during our interview times, both served as incentives for the women to stay in the study. The majority of the women seemed to really enjoy the time we spent together, the friendship, and my interest in their lives. At the final interview I paid the women $15 and gave each woman a bracelet and a small wallet.

Four women in the sample missed their first interview appointment, but I was able to catch up with them within a few days to reschedule the appointment. Over the six month period, there were 14 times that a respondent did not show up for an interview without contacting me to cancel. Six other times respondents informed me ahead of time that they could not make a particular interview date. There were 58 interviews in all.

I continued recruitment throughout the six months in an effort to attain my goal of 12 participants. I began interviewing my first respondent on September 30, 1990 and brought the last woman into my sample on March 8, 1991. Table 1 at the end of this chapter shows the frequency of interviews over the six month data collection period for each of the participants. Names are fictitious.

I asked all the respondents at our final interviews, (except Beatrice and Frieda--who did not have termination interviews), if I could contact them again in early summer to discuss my findings with them. They all agreed they'd like to meet with me again if I could find them.

My methods for staying in contact with participants were very time-consuming, labor intensive and personalized. I am unsure whether such efforts would be feasible in a larger longitudinal study of homeless individuals.

Attrition

I would generally meet women for the first interviews at the shelter at which they were staying or at Angeline's. From there we would usually find a restaurant at which to hold the interview. All the women who met me for the first interview agreed to stay in the study on an ongoing basis. Only one woman who agreed at first to meet with me when approached by shelter staff, later decided she'd rather think about it a while. I saw this woman often during the six months of data collection and she never showed interest in being in the study though she was always very friendly. She was not in the sample of 11 women.

I was surprisingly successful in maintaining contact with my sample. (See Table 1 at the end of this chapter.) One woman, Katy, was recruited into the sample at the end of data collection so I only saw her one time. Another woman, Beatrice, had ongoing excuses for why she couldn't meet with me formally though we had many informal conversations at Angeline's, DESC or on the street. We did meet formally for interviews two times, but with a four month interlude between them. I lost contact with only one woman--Frieda. This was after four interviews spanning a two month period of time. I had termination interviews with eight women at the end of the data collection period. (Frieda wrote me a letter one year after I last saw her to tell me that her partner of 17 years had taken sick and died during the data collection period which was why she had not been available to meet with me.)

Interview Questions, Taping, and Transcribing

Through focused, open-ended questions and nonstandardized interviews (Denzin, 1978), I attempted to enter into the lives of single homeless women in order to understand their lived experiences. In the first interview with each woman I asked about how it was that she came to be without a permanent place of residence. If it felt comfortable to do so, I also asked questions about how she spent her days and where she spent her nights, if she had any source of income, and about her family--both of origin and procreation. At the end of the interview, which generally lasted between a half-hour and an hour, I would pay the woman $5 for her time and set up a time for our next meeting.

Follow-up interviews were devoted to finding out how the woman had spent her time in the time since we had last been together. Prior to each follow-up interview I would review the transcripts from the interview before in order to have specific questions to ask her about her life. I was also generally interested in learning about the following things from all the women and would bring them up when it felt appropriate to do so: what role her informal support system played in her daily life; the formal programs and services she had used; what barriers to service she had encountered; and which programs had benefited her, in her view. I also asked the women questions about substance use; contact with the mental health system; health problems; incidents of physical or sexual assault; relationships with friends, children, lovers, and other family members.

At the first interview I asked each woman if she cared whether I tape recorded our conversation. All the women allowed me to do this once I assured them that the tapes would be confidential. Two women asked me to turn off the tape recorder on one occasion each, while they spoke about particularly sensitive matters. One other woman told me to turn off the tape recorder during an interview in which she appeared to be having a psychotic episode; I refrained from taping my interviews with this particular woman after that episode. Several other interviews with individual woman were not conducive for taping for a variety of reasons: a friend was also in the room; we did the interview while taking a ferry ride; we spent the interview time riding buses. Two times I had technical difficulties with the tape recorder. I took notes immediately after each of the interviews at which I did not tape record.

Over the six month period I did 58 interviews with homeless women. All interviews were transcribed within a few days after the interview. The first few interviews were transcribed word for word, but this proved too time consuming given the resources for this study project. Subsequent interviews were transcribed by paraphrasing the key concepts of the conversations. I selectively transcribed word for word on certain topics that were particularly pertinent or provocative. The nearly sixty hours of taped interviews with homeless women amounted to over 350 pages of single-spaced typed transcripts.

Procedures of Analysis

Analysis of the data began during data collection. I read over transcripts prior to follow-up interviews and began to delimit patterns and themes. Although I worked primarily alone on this research study I was fortunate to have many interested colleagues with whom I could talk about my ideas as they began to develop. Two committee members read through a portion of the transcripts and were able to confirm some of the themes that I found to be emerging; they independently noted similar themes.

My research goals and questions guided the analysis of the data. In examining the question of what the pathways to homelessness were for the women in my sample I again made use of resident experts in qualitative analysis. After summarizing for them the pathways to homelessness of the 11 women in my sample, one committee member-- who has worked extensively with qualitative analysis--and another faculty member--who has had recent experience doing ethnography with low-income women--met with me to discuss themes, patterns and categories that they found in the data. Remarkable agreement existed in the themes that the three of us found in the data.

The analysis has sought to develop concepts, to suggest hypotheses, and to secure a greater understanding about the lives of homeless women as they speak of them. Glaser and Strauss (1967) suggest a method of constant comparative analysis to develop theory from qualitative data. Although theory was not the aim, my analysis has been guided by this technique in that I have arranged themes and patterns into conceptual categories. The evidence that was used to generate these categories has been compared across cases in order to establish the categories' generality and explanatory power.

It is difficult to write down the steps that I used in analyzing the data as it was an ongoing process from the first day of data collection when I immediately became involved in the lives of the women in my sample. As Swanson-Kauffman (1986) has said the process is a reiterative one of reflection and comparison and, for me, discussion with my colleagues:

> Constant reflection on the data gathered to date ensued throughout the entire study. Categories evolved as a result of my living my research study. I found myself constantly

comparing informant to informant, informant to emerging category, category to category, and category to literature reviewed as well as the assumptions with which I began the study. Obviously, the intensity of this reflective process, or as I call it the saturation of the researcher, increased as the data collection ensued. In truth the categories were intuited from ceaseless interaction with the data. (p.64)

Reliability and Validity

Dealing with issues of reliability and validity in qualitative research is somewhat different than it is in quantitative studies. Reliability has to do with the precision of a measuring instrument over repeated measures. One way of assessing the reliability of this study would have been to have another interviewer ask the same questions to see if responses were consistent; limited resources prohibited this reliability check. Another way of assessing the reliability of a piece of qualitative research is through replicating the study. What might be more appropriate in assessing the reliability of a study using a grounded theory methodology would be to apply the theory to another, similar situation to see if it will work to understand this related area of inquiry (Chenitz & Swanson, 1986).

Another important concern in thinking about reliability in qualitative research is whether another coder would code the data in the same way that I do. I made use of two committee members and one outside faculty consultant as a check on my reliability as I developed a system of coding the data.

Validity has to do with accuracy. One method of checking the validity of my data has been to consult with the subjects themselves in order to verify my perceptions and clarify discrepancies throughout data collection.

Glaser and Strauss (1967) link credibility--or validity--of grounded theory to how well the theory "fits" the phenomena under study, whether it has "grab", and it if "works" when put to use. "Fit" means the categories that are generated are indicated by the data and applied readily to the data. "Grab" means the theory speaks to or is relevant to the social world and the persons in that world. Whether it "works" refers to the relevance of the theory to explain, interpret and predict the phenomena under study. Thus the credibility of my research will

Method

depend on whether readers find that it fits, has grab and works when put to use.

Limitations

One obvious limitation of this study is the small size of the sample. This necessarily affects the generalizability of my findings. In grounded theory generalizability or external validity rests on internal variety:

> The greater the range and the variation sought through theoretical sampling, the more certain that the data is [sic] generalizable to other members of the same class or units as the phenomena under study. The greater the internal variety, the greater the likelihood the researcher has sought out and addressed the "negative case", that is the case that does not fit the existing category or proposition. (Chenitz & Swanson, 1986, p. 13)

Because of the difficulty I had in recruiting women into my sample, the internal variety suffered; I never had an option of doing theoretical sampling. I was eager and willing to interview any homeless woman over the age of 45 who was willing to talk to me and did not select among categories.

A related limitation of my sample is a result of both my sampling technique and my time limitations. The women in my sample were women who had access to services and shelters and made use of them. Women who did not use either the shelter system or Angeline's were outside of my sampling domain. Additionally, women who could not read could not have responded to my flyers. And finally, women who do not trust the establishment would be less likely to want to talk with someone they see as a part of it. Therefore my sample of older, homeless women comes from the subsample of homeless women that are in contact with services and are willing to talk with strangers.

Finally, as I was cautioned by service providers before I began, six months was perhaps not a long enough period of time to develop trusting relationships with some of the women--particularly those who had mental health problems. I am unsure if more time would have allowed more trusting relationships to have grown or not, but I am aware that at least one of the women remained very cautious in her disclosure throughout our relationship.

Merves (1986) quotes Thomas and Znaniecki, authors of *The Polish Peasant in Europe and America* in her discussion of the limitations of her ethnographic study of homeless women. She considers the concluding remarks of their study of the Polish peasant--written over fifty years ago--to be equally pertinent to her study, since homeless women are also "subject to either the media's or the public's wrath or pity, but rarely to their understanding" (p.98).

> Our work does not pretend to give any definite and universally valid sociological truths, nor to constitute a permanent model of sociological research; it merely claims to be a monograph, as nearly complete as possible under the circumstances, of a limited social group at a certain period of its evolution, which may suggest studies of other groups, more detailed and more perfect methodologically, thus helping the investigation of modern living societies [homeless people] to rise above its present stage of journalistic impressionism . . . (emphasis added) (quoted in Merves, 1986, p.99)

INTERVIEWS WITH SERVICE PROVIDERS

Sample Selection

A combination of selective sampling (Schatzman & Strauss, 1973) and theoretical sampling (Glaser & Strauss, 1967) guided my selection of service providers. Theoretical sampling happens simultaneously with data analysis. Decisions are made about where to next collect data in order to assure variation in emerging categories.

I began my sampling of key informants by interviewing the service providers that had given me access to their agencies in the first place--generally the director of the program or someone in an administrative position. Part way through data collection, I became interested in interviewing line staff at these agencies because they were perhaps more central in the lives of homeless women. Staff from Health Care for the Homeless also played a major role in the day to day lives of the women in my sample, so I interviewed a nurse and mental health

Method 37

women in my sample, so I interviewed a nurse and mental health worker affiliated with this program. In order to understand more about the opening of the new Women's Shelter I interviewed an administrator from the sponsoring agency--Catholic Community Services. Finally I interviewed the person working in the mayor's office who is most directly involved with the issue of homelessness in the Seattle area. In all, I interviewed 13 service providers. All the interviews took place in the last six weeks of data collection.

Interview Questions

I met with each of the 13 service providers one time. I was interested in learning how services for adult homeless women were perceived by providers. I did not ask service providers about individual women, but rather about: programs as they existed; gaps they saw in services; and about their opinions on how to improve the situation. The approximately 13 hours of taped interviews with service providers came to about 60 pages of single-spaced, typed transcripts.

Procedures of Analysis

The data were analyzed for general themes and ideas. The data from these interviews provided answers to the questions under the fourth research goal presented above. The goal of analysis was to discover the central ideas presented by service providers and to ascertain similarities and differences between what service providers say and what homeless women--the consumers--say.

OBSERVATION

I had originally thought that I might spend an extended period of time with a few of the participants. I did not include this component to my study for two primary reasons. First, because I was able to stay in contact with the women in my sample and was able to meet with most of them on a fairly regular basis, it became less necessary to spend more extended time with any portion of the sample. Secondly, and of greater importance, I felt that such a request would be too great of an intrusion on the privacy of these women and I did not feel comfortable making it.

My original purpose for the ethnographic component--i.e. spending an extended period of time with some of the women--was to learn more about the daily tasks a homeless woman performs to maintain herself; who she approaches for assistance; how she interacts with service providers and the general public and how they in turn react to her; and who she goes to for companionship. I found I was able to obtain answers to some of these questions through meeting women at shelters, spending time with them in restaurants and walking in the streets together to get places. Additionally I spent about 12 hours at Angeline's, at DESC and in the lobby of LCC doing observation.

I spent a total of one and one half hours in the lobby of LCC. I sat in the lobby on two occasions, each time while waiting for a respondent who did not show up for an interview. The lobby is a public meeting place right off the main street, from which homeless men and women staying at the shelter catch an elevator to their respective floors.

I spent a total of about two hours at DESC waiting for participants, writing notes to put up on the bulletin board, looking for particular women. This shelter has several large open rooms, with up to 250 residents walking, sitting, or lying down in them.

The final nine hours were spent at Angeline's. On five occasions I went there specifically to observe for about one and one half hours each time. The remainder of the time I spent at Angeline's was generally while waiting for a homeless woman or service provider before an interview.

My primary purpose for doing this observation was to get a feeling for the places where the women in my sample spent their time. It allowed me a clearer understanding about: the conditions in which they lived; the interactions between service providers and consumers; the rhythms and routines of various agencies; and the way homeless women interact with one another. I believe this understanding strengthened my relationships with the women in my study, thereby allowing me to ask more pertinent questions in the interviews.

Another important reason for this time of observation was to track down missing participants and to make contact with all the sample participants as often as possible, even when in between formal interview times.

PROTECTION OF HUMAN SUBJECTS

Before a woman agreed to be in the study she was carefully informed of the voluntary nature of the research. Each woman was given a consent form to read (or have read to her) and sign at the first interview, and she was given one copy of the signed consent form to keep for herself . Each participant was told that I would try to meet with her on an ongoing basis but that she could pull out of the study at any point in time. I assured the women that they could refuse to answer any question they felt to be too intrusive or uncomfortable. I asked the women at each interview if it bothered them for me to tape record our conversations and their decisions on this matter were respected each time we met.

I assured the women that our conversations were strictly confidential and that their anonymity would be protected. Service provider respondents were given an information sheet explaining the study and assuring confidentiality. In summary, this research respected the rights of the participants and the study was carried out with concern for their dignity and welfare. The study was approved by the University of Washington's Human Subjects Review Committee in July, 1990.

TABLE 1

FREQUENCY OF INTERVIEWS EACH MONTH PER PARTICIPANT
Names are fictitious. Total number of interviews = 58.

	Sept.	Oct.	Nov.	Dec.	Jan.	Feb.	March
Angie	1	1	1	1	1	1	1
Beatrice		1			1		
Carla		1	2		2	2	1
Dierdra		2	1	1	1	2	
Elsie		2	2	2	1	1	1
Frieda		2	1	1			
Gayla			2	1	2		
Hilda			1	2	1	2	
Irene				2	1	1	1
Jackie					1	2	1
Katy							1

CHAPTER 3

SAMPLE DESCRIPTION AND INTRODUCTION TO FINDINGS

INTRODUCTION

This chapter gives a brief demographic sketch of the eleven homeless women in the study. I am unsure of some of the information--especially regarding education level--because certain questions I would not ask directly of the women until we had reached a certain level of trust and that trust was not reached with all the women. Generally I took whatever the women said at face value, although exaggeration was an issue with one woman, lack of understanding due to developmental disability was an issue for another, and a lack of trust, for a third. I note where I have doubts about some information. An introduction to the four chapters on findings follows the sample description.

SAMPLE DESCRIPTION

The eleven women are listed in the order in which I met them and began interviewing them. (See Table 1 at the end of chapter 2.) Names are fictitious.

I met **Angie** in September and we had seven interviews over a 23 week period. She was white and in her late 40's. She had been married and divorced once. Her children by that marriage lived with her former husband's parents. She had had significant love relationships since the marriage--the most recent one with a boyfriend of eight years. Her husband had been Native American and her ex-boyfriend was African American. She had a history of substance abuse and continued to use alcohol at the time of data collection. She had a history of abuse in love relationships and was dealing with that issue in regards to her ex-boyfriend at the time of data collection. She had spent many years in reform school and prison. She had some high school education. Her source of income was through employment. Angie secured housing during the data collection period.

I first interviewed **Beatrice** in early October and we had two interviews over a 17 week period. Our last interview was on January 30, 1991 and we did not have a termination interview because she did not show up for subsequent interviews after January 30. She was white and in her early 60's. She had been married and widowed two times. She had one child who was living independently. I am unsure of her educational level, although I doubt that she finished high school. Nonetheless, Beatrice was quite literate and articulate. She was physically disabled. Her income came from her husband's pension and Supplemental Security Income (SSI).

I first met **Carla** in October and we had 8 interviews over a 22 week period. She was white and in her mid-50's. She had been married and divorced twice and had had significant love relationships since the last marriage. She had two children by her first husband, who was African American; these children were living independently. She had a history of abuse in intimate relationships. She had some high school education but had not graduated from high school. Like Beatrice, she was quite literate and very articulate. She was physically disabled and received her income, during data collection, from General Assistance (GA).

My first interview with **Dierdra** was in October. We had seven interviews over a 21 week period. She was African American and in her mid-50's. She had been married and divorced two times. I believe she had two children--though once she told me that she had three children. The youngest child lived with her aunt and the older one lived independently, I think. She was developmentally disabled and could read very little. I am unsure of her level of education. She had a history of substance abuse but was not using at the time of data collection. Her income came from SSI and she had a payee--that is a caseworker who took responsibility for her check each month.

I met **Elsie** in October and we had nine interviews over a 21 week period. She was Native American and in her mid-40's. She had been married 4 times and divorced 3 times; she was unsure where her fourth husband was. She had had significant love relationships since her last

Sample Description and Introduction to the Findings   43

marriage and, in fact, got involved with a man during data collection with whom she secured housing. She was still with this boyfriend at the end of data collection. She had three children by her second husband--a white man. Two of the children lived independently and one was with relatives. Elsie was prone to exaggeration so I am unsure of her level of education; she claimed to have attended college though I am somewhat doubtful about this. She was physically disabled and received SSI.

I first interviewed **Frieda** in October and we had four interviews over an eight week period. I lost contact with her after her fourth interview on December 6, 1990, and we did not have a termination interview. She was white and in her mid-50's. She had been married three times and divorced twice--she was unsure about where her third husband was. At the time of data collection, she was involved with a man--she called him her "old man"--with whom she'd been spending time for 17 years. During data collection they lived first in a station wagon and later in a camper trailer which they parked illegally on the street. Frieda had no children. She had not completed high school. She was physically disabled and received SSI.

I met **Gayla** in November and we had five interviews over a 15 week period. She was white and in her early 50's. She had been married and divorced one time. She had had significant love relationships since her marriage. She had five children by her marriage and they were all living independently. She had a history of psychiatric hospitalizations but was no longer taking medications. She had some history of abuse in love relationships. She had some college education. She received Social Security Disability Insurance (SSDI) for a psychiatric disability.

I met **Hilda** in November and we had 6 interviews over a 15 week period. She was white and in her late 50's. She had been married and divorced two times. She had four children in all, two by each marriage; they were all living independently. She had had significant love relationships since her last divorce, and recently had left an abusive relationship with a Native American/African American boyfriend. She had a history of substance abuse and was continuing to drink alcohol at the time of data collection. She had not graduated from high school, but had had some vocational training. Hilda secured housing during data collection. Her income was from employment.

I met **Irene** in December and we had five interviews over an 11 week period. She was white and in her late 50's. She was married twice and divorced once. Her second husband--an African American--was institutionalized. She had had love relationships outside of the marriage. At the time of data collection she was trying to leave a 20 year abusive relationship with an African American boyfriend. She had four children by her first husband and they were living independently. She had a history of psychiatric hospitalizations and substance abuse. She no longer took medications nor used drugs or alcohol. She had less than a high school education and was physically disabled. Irene secured housing during data collection. Her income came from her husband's pension.

I met **Jackie** in January and we had four interviews over a six week period. She was African American and in her late 40's. She had been married and divorced one time. She had one child, from that marriage, who was living independently. She had a history of psychiatric hospitalizations but was not taking medications at the time of data collection. I am unsure of her educational level. She received SSD.

I met **Katy** in March at the end of data collection and thus we had only one interview. She was white and in her early 50's. She was unmarried and had one child; this child was in foster care. Katy had a history of psychiatric hospitalizations, but was no longer taking medications. She had some college education. Her income came from SSD.

INTRODUCTION TO FINDINGS CHAPTERS

The following four chapters present the findings from this study on single, older, homeless women.

Chapter 4 presents the women's pathways to homelessness. Chapter 5 discusses their day to day lives. Their future plans and hopes are presented in Chapter 6. Four themes, which emerged from the data, provide the framework for these three chapters. These themes are: relationships, resiliency, normalcy and political awareness. I present my findings by allowing these four themes to emerge from the women's stories of their past, pathways to homelessness; their present, how they live day to day; and their future, their visions for themselves and other homeless women.

Relationships with families of origin, families of procreation, husbands and ex-husbands, lovers and ex-lovers, friends, acquaintances and service providers were pivotal in the women's lives and were

Sample Description and Introduction to the Findings   45

spoken of in every interview. A second theme that appears again and again in the data is that of resiliency in the face of incredible hardship. These women had been dealt some very difficult life circumstances, and yet they proceeded with their lives with a fortitude and sense of humor that often put me to shame. A third theme that emerges from the data is that of trying to maintain a "normal" life despite the extraordinary circumstances of being without a home. The women's efforts to normalize their lives will be particularly evident in the second section which discusses their daily lives, but will also appear in their reporting of their past and their thoughts about the future. And finally the theme of political awareness runs through the data and will be reflected in all three sections. The women were extremely verbal about the oppression they experienced as women, older women, homeless women, disabled women, and impoverished women.

Chapters 4 through 6 related to the first research goal presented in Chapter 2: To learn about the pathways to homelessness for the women in my sample, how they perceive their current situation and future possibilities, and how they spend time on a day to day basis. Questions under this first goal are answered in these three chapters. Additionally, some of the questions under goal number two, concerning informal networks, daily use of services, and housing preferences, are addressed in these chapters.

Chapter 7 presents both the homeless women's views and service providers' views on the services, programs and housing options available to homeless women. This chapter relates to the second and fourth goal presented in Chapter 2. Questions under these two goals will be addressed in the last chapter on findings, chapter 7.

CHAPTER 4

PATHWAYS TO HOMELESSNESS

INTRODUCTION

The women in my sample were all without a permanent place of residence when I first met them. Four of the eleven women secured housing during the six months that I was in contact with them. In the first interview particularly--but also at other times--I asked the women to tell me their stories of how they found themselves to be without a permanent place of residence. Though both their status of being without a home, and the fact that they were 45 or older, were the common characteristics of all the women in my study, individual women did not necessarily think of their homelessness as a primary describing factor. Many of the women had stayed in shelters on and off for years, with periods of being in apartments or rooms in between. In other words their homelessness was cyclical--a term used often by service providers.

Each woman's story is unique, and no pathway is either direct or simple. As the literature suggests there are many causes and correlates to homelessness, and this was true for the older, homeless women making up my sample as well. Poverty and a shortage of affordable, decent housing remain the bottom line issues, but there are other contributing factors. The fact that some of the women in my sample cycle in and out of "permanent" housing situations lends support to the notion that the distinction between homelessness and near homelessness is a blurry one at best. Although four of the 11 women secured housing during the data collection period, staying current on rent payments was difficult for all four of them. When a single incident can jeopardize a marginal housing situation, and put a housed woman into the streets again, it becomes clear that the problem of homelessness is a complex one, and a deep-rooted one, without easy-- or cheap--solutions.

Mental illness, substance abuse, domestic violence, physical illness and/or disability, separation, widowhood or divorce, unemployment or low-wage work, are among the possible entry points for a woman on a pathway toward homelessness. Without financial resources, health insurance, adequate community services, adequately paying jobs or adequate public benefits, these pathways lead to poverty, and, given the lack of affordable housing, eventually to homelessness. Hearing the stories from the women in my sample gave me an appreciation for how these various entry points can be connected in the complicated fabric of a person's life. Yet through the complexity there is a consistent theme: a lack of the financial resources necessary to cushion oneself from destitution each time a difficult life event occurs.

RELATIONSHIPS

At the time of the first interview only one woman was currently with a partner; during data collection one other woman became involved with a man with whom she eventually got an apartment. All but one of the women had been married, most of them more than one time. Most of the women had had other relationships with men after separating from their last husband. I will refer to these men as boyfriends, since that was the term most often used by the women. Ten of the eleven women in the sample had children, though none of them had their children with them at the time of data collection.

The relationship theme was a central component in five of the 11 women's stories about they how they became homeless. Three of these stories involved domestic violence, one concerned the illness and death of a husband, and one centered on a woman's relationship with her daughter.

Three women attributed their current homelessness to trying to get away from an abusive boyfriend. Significantly, these three women were three of the four women who found housing during my data collection period. Briefly I will recount the stories of these women: Angie, Hilda and Irene.

Angie had been involved with one man for eight years. He had been both physically and mentally abusive throughout their relationship. Angie recounted leaving for a period of time each year, but in the past would always go back. When I first met Angie she was living in a shelter; one month later she had kicked her boyfriend out of her old apartment and had moved back in herself. At the end of data collection she was continuing her efforts to keep him out of her life, though this was clearly not an easy task for her. In the years that they had lived together, Angie had been the primary breadwinner, while her boyfriend had done the bulk of the homemaking.

Hilda considered her temporary homelessness to be very unusual for her. She had always had her own home and had worked hard throughout her life to pay the bills. Soon after our first contact, at which time she was living in a shelter, Hilda moved into transitional housing--a community living situation where she could stay up to 3 years. She remained there throughout the period of data collection. She attributed her current life disruption to the event, 18 months earlier, of leaving her alcoholic boyfriend of nine years. She had moved to the Seattle area, where two of her adult children live, shortly after leaving him in order to begin a new life. Problems with drinking and the instability of temporary low wage work have kept her in a financially vulnerable position. At our first meeting she was still clearly grieving the relationship with her boyfriend and feeling lonely for him. She had been the primary breadwinner in the relationship.

Irene had been involved with a man on and off for 20 years. She considered him to be mentally abusive though not physically abusive. Throughout the relationship she had provided the primary financial support--generally from public assistance or pension checks from her husband. In the time that I knew Irene she went from a shelter, to a Single Room Occupancy hotel (SRO), and finally, after the end of data collection, she let me know that she had secured an apartment in subsidized housing.

All three of these women had been the primary breadwinners in the relationships, and after years of abuse had chosen to leave the apartments in which they had lived with their partners. All three women did not expect the partners to continue paying the rent. One eventually kicked her boyfriend out and returned to the apartment, the other two worked to set up new living situations. Interestingly, these women did not gravitate toward shelters for abused women, and one might wonder why they did not take advantage of those services. Only one, Angie, considered the relationship to be physically abusive and she said that she found self-help groups for battered women too depressing. She was doing some independent reading about leaving abusive relationships. Irene had been in a physically abusive relationship at another point in her life and at that point she had taken advantage of a shelter for battered women; she did not consider herself a battered woman now. She was getting counseling from Health Care for the Homeless around leaving her most recent relationship.

Beatrice's story is different, but a marital relationship and her role as a caregiving wife are its central components. Beatrice's problem with homelessness first started with her husband's death, six years before data collection. Up until her mid-fifties, Beatrice had lived a relatively stable life with employment and housing. Her husband was quite ill in the last two years of his life, and Beatrice eventually needed to stop working in order to be a full-time caregiver. Her husband did not have health insurance and his illness left her with many bills. She had spent the last six years using her small social security check to make payments on these bills. Beatrice lost her housing security with the financial crisis caused by her husband's long-term illness and death which left her with bills and a dramatic reduction in income.

Though Jackie's homelessness might be attributed to her mental illness, she traced her homelessness to being kicked out of her daughter's house seven years ago. Since that time she had been traveling and living in shelters, generally spending her social security check fairly quickly at the beginning of the month. Jackie did not blame her daughter for wanting to live an independent life and appeared to hold no malice toward her daughter for her present situation. She said:

> Well my daughter decided when she got married--she was in a common law marriage--she said "Momma go and don't come back". And I understood, my own mother came in between me and my daughter. When I come it upsets the apple cart. Every house has their way, the house rules and game plan. I was hoping to mold her into my house rules, but with the second generation. . . . So I just decided not to go back to New York and I wanted to do some traveling.

As mentioned earlier, all but one of the women in the sample had children. Some of these children were adults, living independently, and some were minors living with relatives. Most of these children were financially struggling themselves and none of the women felt their children should be supporting them nor bail them out of their homeless situations. As Hilda says:

> My children have problems of their own. They do not need their mother to be dragging their back side. . . . I do think that it is bloody unfortunate that you can work all your life and nobody cares. Obviously my kids care but they don't need their mother dumped on them.

Gayla didn't like it when people wondered why her children didn't take her in:

> I have five children. I don't like it when people say how can your children let you live this way. It's not fair. I didn't raise my children thinking that some day they could take care of me.

In summary, five women considered intimate relationships to be important in describing how they had become homeless. Four of the women in the sample considered disruption in their relationships with partners to have played significant roles in their current homelessness. One woman attributed her homelessness to separating from her daughter, although she seemed to hold no malice toward her daughter. Additionally, several of the women were adamant in saying that they did not blame their children for their homelessness, and did not like it when other people insinuated that their children should take care of them.

RESILIENCY

Resiliency, the second theme to be discussed in this section on pathways to homelessness, emerged from the voices of the women when they spoke of their childhoods. Four of the women described very difficult childhoods. Six others spoke less negatively about their childhoods. Of these six, two retained some positive relationships with their families of origin, but current relationships for the remaining four were weak, nonexistent or hurtful. I learned nothing about one woman's family of origin because I only saw her two times and we had not reached a level of trust to talk about her childhood in those two interviews. None of the women had living biological parents with whom they were in contact. Three had living foster parents or adoptive parents about whom they occasionally spoke, though these people were not a part of the women's daily lives at the time I knew them.

One common view among service providers is that single, adult homeless women tend to come from very difficult backgrounds in which they have experienced a great deal of abuse. What is perhaps more remarkable than that they have had such challenging early lives, is that they have survived these situations so courageously and without self-pity.

Angie spoke of her childhood in a very matter of fact way. She saw it as the beginning of a history of the drug and alcohol abuse that continued to plague her life. She wondered if there was a connection between her childhood and her willingness to stay in an abusive relationship so long.

> I still don't know why I let myself go through it.... I'm thinking about going to see a therapist. When I was 12 I went to reform school because my mother had an illegitimate baby. It sounds so preposterous nowadays. But that was 35 years ago. They locked me up. I did five years in reform school. Then I went to the penitentiary because I got involved in drugs. I don't have happy memories of my childhood. I don't have any memories really. I thought a therapist could help open that up and help me understand who I am now.

And yet she did not dwell on the hard times she had had as a child nor did she allow it to keep her from feeling good about herself and her life. One day we were talking about labels that are used to describe behaviors and families and Angie said:

> The one I don't like is "dysfunctional family",. Everyone had a dysfunctional family. What's functional? There aren't any normal people that I know.

Though Carla did not attribute her homelessness to her hard childhood, she did think it had contributed to her feelings about herself:

> I was born in '36 and he (Swedish father) came over during the gold rush to Nome, Alaska. I ended up in an orphanage in '38 and I was separated from my brother which I think caused a lot of traumatic problems. And my foster mother and father were not able to give the kind of love and assurance that I needed. The kind of love they gave me was that they would buy me things. I don't ever remember them hugging me or kissing me or telling me that they loved me. Instead I felt that I was inferior which was the worst thing they could have done.... One time I used my father's toothbrush by mistake and he hit me. I apologized and he said I deserved it. And then they talked bad about my biological parents.

But she had forgiven these people and learned how to deal with their negative attitudes since they remained marginally in her life.

> They can be upsetting. They always see the negative side. You need to ignore it and come back with something positive.... I don't have any malice. I'm over that. They have problems that they never overcame. I can't judge them. They probably tried to love me. They are 97 years old and you have to forgive them.

Elsie was physically disabled and had been since childhood. Because her stories about her childhood varied from severe neglect to luxurious adventure, it was often difficult to know which portion of her stories was true and which portion was a part of a make believe world she had created. During one interview she told me that her adoptive mother was a horrible person who left her on the door step of a hospital for disabled children where she then stayed for five years. Later in the interview she claimed to have lived all over the world as a child, going to the best schools. Elsie was a fun loving and spontaneous woman who seemed to use tall tale fabrication as a way to make an otherwise hard life easier to live and enjoy. While in several interviews sheclaimed to be the niece of comedian Red Skelton, and to be related to the famous Native American, Geronimo, at other times she said that she had no relations.

> Nobody is related to me. I don't have no relatives. I'm the oldest in the family. My mother died when I was born I guess. My real dad died in the second world war. He died in 1944. Then I was adopted out. But anyway I'm OK. I've got everything together. If I get my check I'll feel great.

Whatever may be the actual true story, Elsie made the most of her situation and found and created much joy in her life.

The resourcefulness and fortitude that the women constantly exhibited was evident when they talked about the recent circumstances that had brought them to homelessness. The resiliency theme appears in the stories of Frieda and Beatrice.

Frieda and her boyfriend of 17 years were physically disabled. Frieda received SSI and her boyfriend got a smaller General Assistance check--not having been granted SSI. With these combined checks they tried to make ends meet. When I met Frieda, she and her "old man" were living in a station wagon. They had been living in it for several months, after having been evicted from a substandard apartment. Originally they had agreed to do some repairs on this apartment in exchange for a reduction in the rent. It took the landlord seven months to get them the materials to do the repairs at which time Frieda and her boyfriend were in such poor health that they could not do the physical work. The landlord chose to charge them to have the work done, so Frieda stopped paying rent. Frieda told her story of how she and her "old man" dealt with these slum lords:

> We were there about a year. During the course of that year they raised the rent three times plus we paid our own lights and gas. After seven months they came in and fixed the bathroom sink and the kitchen light. Still they said they didn't have the materials to finish the apartment. Finally we went over and we said "Look when are you going to get the materials?". But by this time both our healths had deteriorated. We said "We just can't afford to do it now--we are not up to par to do it". [The landlord said] "Well then I'll have to have someone come in and you'll have to pay $200 to have it

done". There were gaps in the wall, the ceilings needed to be redone. It was in horrid shape. We said "We aren't paying another $200, this is suppose to be the apartment people's job". We said "That's it, we aren't paying no more rent".

Eventually they were evicted for nonpayment of rent but they won their case against the landlord when they described the apartment's conditions to the judge. They doubled up with friends for awhile but the mix of personalities in tight quarters became too uncomfortable.

So we left there and immediately went out to a used car lot and we saw this car. We asked them how much it was and they told us. We said we only have so much we could pay down and we explained our situation that we only get so much each month. They gave us credit for 2 months and we finished paying it off. So we got that and we've been living in a station wagon ever since.

Frieda had an openness and friendliness about her that was contagious. Despite her debilitating physical condition and her incredibly cramped quarters, she was cheery and jovial. As winter set in, her chronic lung disease became worse with the onset of a cold. Recuperation from sickness is difficult when you live in a car. When I asked her if her sickness was slowing her down at all she replied:

No I keep going. I can't afford to slow down. If I slow down I'll just fall over and give it up. As long as I have some life left in me I'm going to take full advantage of it.

Her resiliency and personal courage were reflected in her philosophy of life:

Why not enjoy life while you can. Why worry about what might happen tomorrow. It might never get here. Enjoy today.

Beatrice was left with many bills after her husband died. She told me how she took charge of the situation and did the best she could given the circumstances:

There were so many instances where he'd borrow one hundred here or two hundred there. God knows the amount. He just had me crackers. He was a drunk on top of that. When he died I went straight down to the bank and we had 680 something dollars and I drew out everything. I had them write me a money order and put it in my bag and came downtown and opened another account and dropped the money in there. And then just started paying off these hundred dollar accounts he had with people. Then the other bills like the phone bill and the light bill. This and that and the other.... We had a phone bill of $378 or whatever it was because I was in touch with my sister-in-law back in Staten Island quite a bit in those days and I paid the phone bill in $10 payments. They must have hated me because I'd send them ten stinking dollars. But I got the phone bill paid up. Hey it wasn't any fun. I would get $268.78 from his company insurance and I was getting $44 a month from SSI and I was getting, when they cut it off, $92 a month from the years he spent in the service.

Beatrice was able to pay off these bills by living in a shelter and not paying rent. She worked for a few years after her husband's death doing home health care until she had an accident that left her unable to do that sort of work any longer. She was proud of having paid back the bills and seemingly happy with her life. She had no regrets and wanted no pity:

I make it. I make it all the time. I'm just lucky...when he got sick, we made it. It was OK. We had a wonderful life, and I liked him too. He was OK. I'd do the same damn thing over again.

The women did not dwell on the hard times they had had. They generally were proud of the efforts they had made through life to deal with the challenges which they had been dealt. Keeping a positive attitude about life was of utmost importance to most of them.

NORMALCY

The normalcy theme that runs through the data serves to challenge myths that depict older, homeless women as eccentric bag women. This theme will be particularly evident in the next chapter on the women's day to day lives, but it is also important in understanding how these women came to be without permanent places of residence. There are two ways of thinking about the normalcy theme in this section: 1) the events that had led to the women's circumstances happen to everyone and are not particularly extraordinary; and 2) the way women handle these events is how one would expect "normal" people to deal with difficult situations.

For example, Hilda and Irene mentioned above, left their homes in order to be free of abusive love relationships. Women do this all the time and generally this is seen as a proactive and healthy action.

Hilda in her decision to turn over a new leaf decided to leave California in order to come and live with a grown daughter and her family in the Seattle area. She eventually had to leave her daughter's home since the commute into Seattle for her employment was too long. One primary reason that she remained in shelters and then in transitional housing rather than in her own apartment, which she would have preferred, was that she had to depend on erratic, temporary work at low wages for many months.

She experienced wage discrimination in her efforts to find work, and finally settled on a permanent part-time position at very low wages. At one point in data collection, after she had been terminated from a temporary job which she had been hopeful would be permanent, she discussed how age discrimination was affecting her success in securing a job now though she had worked all her life:

> I don't mean to feel miserable, but it is awfully hard. I've worked damn hard all my life. I've never shirked work. I've tried really hard to always keep in work. People my age, they don't want to bother with me. You know what? It is dumb, because at my work I can really. . . . well. . . . I'm steady and I know a lot. This thing about getting teens in. . . . they don't know what they are doing. It hurts. . . . Hey, I'm only 59 and I have a lot of life left and I'm a good worker.

Irene left her abusive relationship and went to a shelter for families and single women. She began to take advantage of education and training programs for homeless individuals. These activities, along with weekly visits to a counselor with Health Care for the Homeless, helped her to maintain her independence from her abusive boyfriend. When life at the shelter became too difficult due to drug abuse by one of the residents, she moved to an SRO, though this was very difficult for her financially. Given her own history of drug abuse she made the decision to leave what felt like an unhealthy living situation, in order to have more control over her living space. Paying more than half of her monthly check for rent in order to live in this tiny SRO, left her living a very marginal life, but it did bring her peace of mind.

Gayla had a history of mental illness and thus one might expect her to more easily fit into the stereotype of the crazy disheveled woman pushing a shopping cart around the streets of the city. In fact, Gayla was an attractive woman who cared how she looked and was always quite fashionably and neatly dressed. Her pathway to homelessness began with a nervous breakdown in her mid-forties. She had spent most of her adult life living in an upper-middle class neighborhood, and prior to her breakdown had owned a large home where she was living with her children. At the time of the breakdown she had been divorced from a wealthy man for many years and alimony had been terminated; she was working four jobs to make ends meet. One role that she spoke of frequently was that of being a foster mother, something she did for many years after her divorce and before her hospitalization.

Gayla spent five years as a psychiatric inpatient at various institutions around the state. Three years before I met Gayla she had diagnosed herself as recovered and left the last psychiatric institution in which she had resided--a half-way house. She received Social Security Disability Insurance (SSDI) but preferred working. She felt that she experienced discrimination in her search for employment due to her former disability as a psychiatric patient. She felt in a "catch-22" situation because she would have liked to work and be independent but she couldn't give up her Social Security--which she got for her psychiatric condition--until she had steady work:

> I can't get a good job and keep it. The very people that have been paid to wean people, Social Security, are the only people

who are calling me disabled. When I found discrimination I was afraid to not be called disabled because I needed Social Security until I could get work.

Gayla had been without a home a good portion of the time since her release from the half-way house. She may have been eligible for subsidized housing given her status as a disabled woman, but she was uncomfortable with that label and found the available housing unappealing. Throughout her three years of intermittent homelessness she had been actively looking and interviewing for work. She had secured several temporary positions doing home health care, but had not been able to find permanent employment. She attributed this lack of success to discrimination.

Gayla's homelessness was partially a result of the very normal desire to have employment and to live in a clean, safe apartment in a neighborhood in which she was comfortable. She did not feel she was disabled and she was angry at being labeled so. Given our society's emphasis on self-sufficiency and independence, it is understandable that she would choose employment over receiving a check for a disability she did not think she had. Her refusal to move into available subsidized housing is also very normal as the conditions were distasteful and frightening to her.

Dierdra was developmentally disabled and her stories were always given to me in bits and pieces that did not necessarily fit together well. I never got a clear picture of the direct path that brought her to live in a shelter. She had a caseworker who served as the payee for her SSI check, and throughout the period of data collection she claimed that this person was trying to get her into one housing situation or another, whenever an apartment or room opened up.

She had lived with her mother at one time but her mother had recently died, so she could no longer live there. Her son was living with her aunt, but I assumed there was not room enough for Dierdra to live there, and perhaps more importantly, she preferred her independence. She had lived in a subsidized apartment once, but had not been able to maintain it when she chose to go on a trip to Mississippi with her family for a big family reunion. At one time she had lived in a treatment facility for drug and alcohol abuse. She no longer used substances.

A family death, a family reunion, and substance abuse are all fairly frequent occurrences in a person's life. But with minimal income (about $400/month), the shortage of subsidized housing and a chronic disability, it was difficult for Dierdra to maintain a permanent residence. When I tried to get a clearer picture of why she had stopped living at her last subsidized apartment she gave me these responses:

> I moved out because I was sick. My sister was moving to another place and I had to walk up that hill. There was good reason, nothing bad, we were talking about going to Mississippi and stuff.... I left everything down there. They didn't put me out.

She said they moved someone into her apartment while she was gone and she lost some of her belongings. She dealt with her homeless situation in the best way she knew to:

> I didn't know about the Morrison [DESC] so I went down to Angeline's and they told me about the Morrison. Stayed outside a couple times, even lived in a garbage can for a while. Me and a friend.

While life at a shelter or sleeping in a dumpster is not normal for most individuals, Dierdra's options were limited and these choices did allow Dierdra to maintain a certain degree of independence. With the characteristic resiliency exhibited by all the women, she always did her best to take care of her basic physical and social needs, she was always looking to improve her situation--very normal behavior given the circumstances.

POLITICAL AWARENESS

Throughout data collection I was struck by the fact that the women tended not to blame themselves for their homeless situation. There was an awareness of the inequities in our society and of the discrimination to which they were subjected. With the exception of several women wondering why they had allowed themselves to remain so long in abusive relationships, there was little talk of self blame or inadequacy. This political astuteness can be seen in several of the examples already discussed: Frieda's refusal to pay rent to a landlord who was providing inadequate housing; Hilda's awareness that her difficulty in locating employment was a function of age discrimination; and Gayla's analysis of the social security system and its inability to help her gain independence.

Carla's pathway to homelessness had been a complicated one in which she had run into many barriers. She was very aware of being oppressed as an impoverished, disabled, older woman with little education.

Carla attributed her homelessness to problems with her back which had begun in her thirties when she had had multiple, problem pregnancies. She was angry that she had not been able to have abortions back then, and angry that the right to abortion was in danger again. During her last pregnancy she had lost so much blood that she had been considered dead at one point.

> Thank God I woke up. But I don't know how many women died that way because they didn't have a right to an abortion. I think that it should be between a woman and her doctor. That last child I had--the baby--died anyway. The doctor told me that there was something wrong with the pregnancy in the first three months and that I should have a legal abortion. He knew the danger. It was so difficult for a woman to get an abortion that doctors were scared to death to help a woman even though they knew that her life was in danger and that the baby wouldn't be healthy. Now isn't that crazy? And they are trying to do that again. They're trying to do it again! They're nuts. If you don't want to have an abortion you don't have to have an abortion. But the ones that need them--it is between the woman and her doctor.

Carla eventually left her husband who was physically abusive and went to California with her two children. She went on welfare and tried to make a go of it. She continued to have back problems, eventually requiring major surgery. Her husband never sent her child support. At one point she was so sick that she sent her children back to their father, but they soon returned to her when he was physically abusive to them.

Her analysis of her situation as a struggling single mother reflects her understanding of the sexism so prevalent in our society and social welfare policies:

> The political process works against the woman and against the children for the political arena. . . . I was so sick and in pain and having to use codeine and everything and they had no idea what was wrong with me. I was so broke, so depressed financially. So I sent both my kids to stay with their dad because of course he had money and he had a nice home and he had everything. He never had to pay for anything. He never lost himself. He was living it up the whole time, and some social worker said "Oh that's OK". He called me up one time and told me that a social worker told him that if he gave me $35 a month that would be fine and laughed. Called me on the phone, here I am with two little kids, I'd lost my health, I'm caught with $300 debt. I went through hell. I sent them to stay with their dad because I didn't have a car, I didn't have any money, I was sick. That really upset both my kids and myself.

At the time of data collection, Carla's children were grown and they lived independently. Carla received General Assistance and had been trying for several years to get SSI. She tried to work, but generally after about two weeks her back would become too sore for her to continue.

> What happens is that I've tried to go back to work well about six times. What happens is that within two weeks of sitting up I start getting this pressure back here and pain in my head and down in Tacoma I tried for two and a half weeks until I felt that my hip was going numb. I said I'm killing myself for what? A part time job that doesn't offer medical care? I said the hell with it.

But when she quit her last job and went to a doctor she got a reaction which she considered typical. She did not feel as though she were taken as seriously by doctors or the social security system as a man in a similar situation would be.

> I told this doctor that I'd been in bed for 10 days and I told him my background and he said well you've been dealing with it for this long, you're doing OK. If I was a man and I had told that guy that I had to be in bed for 10 days and couldn't work, he would have had a different attitude. There is so much prejudice against women. Some men really think that women aren't suppose to work. They think that you should be with your husband.

Similarly, her experience with Social Security had been frustrating. They were unwilling to give her SSI for her back as no one was able to say definitively that she could not work. At one point someone in Social Security suggested that she go back to work as an employment counselor. She found this suggestion to be condescending since she would have loved to be an employment counselor, but she lacked the credentials to be hired as one, even if she were physically able.

> Does anyone really believe that I would be living here, I've lost everything that I've ever had. You can't keep any clothes. It's ridiculous to think that someone would just not want to work. I'm not an alcoholic, so what would be the reason?.... They thought I could go back to work as an employment counselor.... it's insane really. I wish that I could go back to work as an employment counselor. Get some nice clothes. That's a good job. Have a life.

Carla had been homeless on and off for a couple of years. Her life cycled between working and trying to get SSI. She would try to work for awhile until her back problem made that prohibitive, then she would try to get SSI until that became too frustrating, so she would go back to work. She gave me a description of this cycle when I asked her to tell me why she was without a permanent place of residence.

> I'm not able to work now. I'm trying to get SSI and boy do they lie and cheat and pull everything in the books on you. They sure take money out of your check fast enough, but when you need help, boy they just out and out lie. Last time.... I tried once before to get on SSI and gave up and went back to work part time and all I've been able to do for

the past six years is part time on telephones. And that is hard work.

The themes of relationships, resiliency, normalcy and political awareness appeared over and over again in the women's stories about their past and about how they became homeless. These themes emerged again in the women's descriptions of their day to day lives over the months that I knew them. Using relationships, resiliency, normalcy and political awareness as a backdrop, Chapter 5 discusses the women's daily lives.

CHAPTER 5

DAY TO DAY LIVES

INTRODUCTION

    I learned about the women's day to day lives in a number of ways. In each of the follow-up interviews I would ask the women to tell me about how they had spent their time since our last interview. I would ask them specific questions about particular issues which we had discussed in the previous interview to get an update on how these issues were continuing to affect their lives. These topics included employment, housing, relationships, health, money, and emotional status. At each interview I would ask the woman how she had spent her day so far and what her plans were for the rest of the day. On a number of occasions I would ask a woman how she had spent the preceding day from start to finish.

    The goal of learning about the women's day to day lives was to gain an understanding of how homeless women cope in practical ways with their homeless condition. As I became involved in these women's lives I realized that "coping" was an outsider's perspective. The women were living their lives unselfconsciously, but resiliently. Many did not label themselves as homeless, and in fact were not homeless part way through data collection. All the women had many facets to their lives over and above the fact that they lived--or had lived--in shelters. Our conversations in follow-up interviews went where the women took them and often touched on many far reaching subjects.

RELATIONSHIPS

One persistent stereotype of older homeless women is that they are isolated and without social contacts or networks. This stereotype places homeless women outside normative behavior particularly because the lives of women in our culture generally do revolve around relationships. The women in my sample did not fit this myth of living lonely, isolated existences, but rather appeared very normal in their roles as mothers, lovers, friends, and daughters. Like women elsewhere in our culture, much of their energy was devoted to worrying about and taking care of the people in their lives.

All but two of the women in my sample were very strongly identified as mothers and talked considerably about their children. For the two that did not do so, one had not had children and the other was not in close contact with her son. The women's relationships with their children tended to be complicated, bringing them both joy and pain-- something that is hardly unusual for parent-child relationships. The five women discussed below exemplify how the women's children were a part of their day to day lives.

Hilda's relationship with her four children was perhaps the least rocky and the most supportive on a day to day basis. Hilda had four grown children, three with families of their own. She became a great grandmother while I knew her. One of her children lived out of the country, one lived out of state and the last two were in the Seattle area, though some distance from where she lived. She spoke with the two in the Seattle area almost daily and was in regular correspondence contact with the other two. She was interested in their lives and concerned about them. She enjoyed spending time with them when she could, especially at the holidays, but had no desire to live with them.

The only times that I knew Hilda to feel badly about her relationships with her children was when she was drinking; one daughter did not like to have much to do with her during those periods. She also felt that her children had little understanding for the grieving she was doing for the alcoholic, abusive boyfriend she had left 18 months earlier. Every time that I saw Hilda she was knitting something new for one of her children or grandchildren.

Irene's relationships with her children were more troubled and she worried about them constantly. Three of her four children had been taken from her when she was hospitalized for a nervous breakdown more than 20 years ago and when their father--her husband at the time--was in prison. She had not seen two of these children since they were small though she knew where they were and she was making efforts to be back in contact with them. The third child was in prison--something she learned by chance--and she had visited him one time and was planning another trip. Her fourth and youngest child was taken from her due to her alcoholism about 10 years earlier. This child lived independently in Seattle at the time of data collection and had psychiatric problems. He was abusive to her when she tried to make contact with him and she worried about him a lot.

Though Irene's relationships with her children had been difficult and erratic she wanted very much to be in contact again and to try to rebuild friendships now that she was living a more stable life. Each time I saw her she spoke of her plans to see her son in prison, or of writing a card or letter to one her children, or of seeing her youngest son by chance and how he had treated her. I believe this focus on her children had intensified since leaving the abusive relationships with her boyfriend, and would possibly result in closer ties with them in the future.

Carla had two grown children. At the time of data collection she was out of communication with her daughter, who lived in Seattle. She spent quite a bit of time with her son, who lived in a city an hour's bus ride away. Her relationship with her son was up and down throughout the data collection period. She would often spend weekends with him at his apartment in order to be able to rest her back injury. She took him food from the food bank and did housecleaning and laundry while she was there. Throughout data collection she was considering moving in with him and her feelings about that idea fluctuated depending on their current relationship. She related some of her conflicted feelings about her children in the first interview:

> My daughter and I are not speaking because.... I married a black man when people just didn't do that.... It is funny how it affected my kids. My daughter looks like her dad and she relates to being black, and my son looks like me and he relates to being white. So our family is cut right down the middle now and I don't know what to do about it. I was staying at my son's for the weekend. His sister and I had an upset and we've not been talking for a while. I love her. He doesn't want me to

ever make up with her. He wants us to put her out of our lives. That's not right.... My son is 30 and my daughter is 28. I'm at a point where I just can't deal with it anymore so I'm going to wait. Maybe in two or three years my son will grow up a little. The way I think, your flesh and blood is your flesh and blood. But then I talked with a social worker who said she thought that staying away from my daughter sounded like a good idea. She has been abusive. I'd like for the three of us to go to a psychiatrist. We have a serious problem.

When things weren't going well with her son, Carla would talk about leaving the area in order to get some distance from her children. She felt very emotionally entangled with them even when she didn't see them. Although she did not talk with her daughter throughout the data collection period she expected to be back in contact with her once her daughter had grown up some. Her relationship with her son, while having its ups and downs, did provide her some respite from shelter life and an ongoing connection with family. (Carla did in fact reconnect with her daughter several months after data collection, when her daughter was ill and Carla helped to take care of her.)

Gayla was in contact with her five children though she didn't let them know exactly where she was staying. She thought this would upset them. The time she spent with her only grandchild was her most precious time and she believed it helped to keep her going. She was very protective of her "past life" as she called it--which included her children and grandchildren--and felt that staff in the shelters and social security personnel were trying to take it away from her by seeing her only as a homeless woman who had once been hospitalized for a psychiatric condition.

Once she told me about returning late to the shelter after spending time with her grandson. She was so protective and secretive of that time that she wouldn't tell staff why she was late:

That is the joy of having children--being a grandmother.... I really wanted to see my grandson, I hadn't seen him in three weeks.... yeah and that intimidates people that I have a past life. I tell people they are not my past life, they are my present life and my future.... and I say you are not about to destroy that.... I had a late pass because of taking care of my grandson. My daughter works every other weekend. The reason I was late was because I got to see his first secondary tooth. I never get to talk about my grandson with my daughter when he isn't around and he is so sensitive. I never get to talk about his heart murmur. . . . I'd rather be barred [banned from shelter] than share that with someone who hates my guts.

Katy was living in a shelter and her daughter was in foster care. Katy longed for the time that she would be reunited with her daughter. She was in daily contact with her daughter on the phone, and she saw her several times a week. Katy's daughter had recently gotten pregnant and thought that she, Katy and the new baby could get an apartment together. Katy was unsure that welfare would allow that to happen since her daughter was only 16. She would have loved for them all to be living together. Her fantasy was to be able to take care of the grandchild while her daughter finished high school, something Katy knew her daughter needed to do, especially now that she was going to be a mother.

Relationships with parents were less central in the women's lives. Many of the women had had adoptive or foster parents and most of the women's parents--both biological and otherwise--had died. Three women had surviving parents that were not a part of their daily lives. Only Carla mentioned contact with her parents during the data collection period. These were foster parents with whom Carla had had a difficult childhood. At the time of data collection they lived a couple of hours outside of Seattle in a retirement home. Her foster father died during the data collection period and this caused Carla considerable anguish. She felt guilty for not having spent more time with him and angry that more efforts weren't made to save his life. She thought that she could have convinced him to live, though he was 90 years old and very sickly. She did not think that people understood just how valuable older people were. She believed that the staff at the retirement community, the doctors and his family had failed him. She now felt responsible to check up on her foster mother, though this was difficult for her to do without a car. Her foster parents had a biological son who was much better off financially than was Carla, and yet she felt she had as much responsibility for taking care of these older people as this wealthy son had. She had forgiven these people who had been quite abusive to her in her childhood.

Love relationships with men were important for five of the women. The other six women rarely, if ever, spoke of boyfriends. Three of the women who frequently spoke of boyfriends--Angie, Hilda and Irene--had recently left abusive relationships. Angie and Irene had ongoing contact with their ex-boyfriends which caused them both considerable anxiety. Hilda missed her ex-boyfriend but did not know where he was.

Two women had current boyfriends. Frieda had been living with her "old man" for 17 years and Elsie met her boyfriend at the beginning of data collection and began to live with him a month later. Frieda and her "old man" went everywhere and did everything together. They seemed to really enjoy each other's company and spent a lot of time alone together.

> We aren't too much into crowds. We prefer to be by ourselves.... we usually go everywhere together, in fact we'd be together right now if you'd let him.... after 17 years you get pretty use to each other.

When I first met Elsie, she was living at DESC and spent most of her time surrounded by lots of men. She talked of all the friends she had and how all the men were jealous of one another because of her. One month into data collection she became involved with one man at the shelter and they decided to get an apartment together. This move caused her life to change dramatically. Although she would come downtown daily to pick up mail and do other errands, she spent almost all of her time with her boyfriend. Her boyfriend was very possessive and became very jealous of any time she spent with other men. She said that her friends didn't like her boyfriend and his friends didn't like her. Sometimes she said that she missed her freedom and being with lots of people and other times she said that her life with her boyfriend suited her just fine. At the end of the data collection period she had become payee for her boyfriend's SSDI check. She wasn't sure if this was going to make her feel trapped in the relationship.

Many of the women had friends upon whom they depended for support, company, and sharing of material items. When I first met Angie she was living in a shelter after leaving her abusive boyfriend. Eventually she kicked her boyfriend out of her apartment and moved back into it herself. Though the apartment was a small efficiency apartment, she always had at least one other person living there with her. For months she slept on the couch while she allowed a male friend, who had recently gotten out of jail and who had no place to go, to have her bed. During part of that time another friend was homeless, so she allowed this woman and her boyfriend to come live with her too. During a snow storm that stopped the city for about a week she said that she had six people living in her apartment. When I mentioned to her how generous I thought she was, she said: "Well you know there have been times when I wished that someone had done that for me."

Beatrice and Dierdra were two women who had "lived" at DESC for years. They were two very independent women who didn't necessarily spend that much time together, but it was clear that they looked out for one another. Beatrice seemed to avoid meeting with me formally but one time showed up with Dierdra and said that we should all go out together. At that meeting we planned to do things together from then on, but Beatrice always had an excuse for not coming to subsequent dates. Dierdra would always wrap up some of her breakfast to take to Beatrice after our interviews. When I asked them if they would like to be neighbors if they could both get subsidized housing, they both emphatically said no, but Beatrice then countered with one of her many sayings: "But I notice that when the hair is short that we are right there."

Part of showing friendship was giving gifts and sharing. Dierdra often spoke of sharing with Beatrice when she had something extra and Beatrice did the same for Dierdra. Dierdra also shared with other women in the shelter, and though she might not know their names or anything about them, a sort of friendship would be established. Once I asked her how she was spending her time while she was sick and on "bed rest" at the shelter. She said: "I talk to the lady next to me. She buys candy and stuff and she shares with me and I share with her." Many of the women gave me small gifts throughout the data collection period, often saying something like "You always give something to me, so I want to give you something too."

Finally, some women established friendships with service providers. Angie became quite close with one counselor at the shelter before moving back to her apartment and would occasionally go back to see her, or call her on the phone during the months of data collection. This counselor even suggested Angie apply for her counselor job when she was leaving the agency.

Irene was good friends with her General Equivalency Diploma (GED) teacher and depended on that support as she tried to stay away from her abusive boyfriend.

> My teacher is really good. She has been a lot of help to me. She knew that I needed to get away from my boyfriend, so she took time away from school to help me move my stuff. We moved it over to the school until we could find a place to move it.

Irene would often go over to Angeline's during the day to have a sandwich and to talk with the staff there even when she did not have a formal appointment with her counselor. She talked about trying to quit smoking just as her counselor was doing and using the fact that they would be doing it together as a primary motivator for making this difficult change in her life.

RESILIENCY

When I first thought about doing this research project and I spoke with service providers about the best way to meet with women and learn about their lives, I was told time and time again that these women were busy and that I would need to make it worth their while to spend time with me--thus the small financial compensation. Over the data collection period, I did indeed learn to appreciate how difficult their lives were and how ingenious the women were in getting their needs met. Day to day life was hard and it was with resiliency that the women kept on going, doing what they needed to do, and generally with good humor.

Though I only saw Beatrice two times for formal interviews I did see her frequently at Angeline's or DESC or on the street waiting for a bus. I would chat with her at these times in order to get an understanding about her life. She was often sick with bronchial pneumonia which she said was difficult to get rid of when living in the shelter. Her health and her trips to various doctors seemed to be central in her life. Some of her medical problems originated from the time she was hit in the head by a pipe that had fallen off the building outside of the DESC. Since that time she had been unable to work. Her attitude was a courageous one:

But I've had a good life. I thought I must have done something. Because what goes around comes around. I needed a good hit in the head or something. I don't know what happened. But it all worked out. And I'm proud and happy that I've managed to keep my medical going and my appointments current. And keep the coupons current without one bit of help. Anyway. And that is the way I like it--when they owe me, Honey.

Two incidents occurred in Dierdra's life while I knew her that demonstrated to me how challenging her life was as a homeless woman. Several months after I met Dierdra she was hospitalized for emergency surgery on one of her breasts. I visited her in the hospital and asked about where she would go when she was discharged. She wanted to stay in the hospital as long as possible since the prospect of returning to the shelter was not appealing. When I asked her if she would be returning to DESC she said:

Not yet, not until it heals up. All those men sitting in the middle of the floor. You'd bump yourself on the bed down there. You can't bump yourself here, the beds are soft.

She did in fact return to DESC, probably sooner than she would have liked.

The last time I saw Dierdra she was dealing with another crisis. Almost all of her clothes had been stolen two days earlier. When I asked her how she had been spending her time, understandably, everything centered on the fact that she didn't have any clothes. She had spent the previous two days being mad, looking for clothes and washing the few clothes that she did have. When I asked her how she was going to spend the rest of the day, she mentioned going to sleep early that night since she needed to rest up for another day of being without, and looking for, clothes.

Carla's life evolved around taking care of her back. Some days she could not get out of bed at all and she would either go to her son's for a few days, if they were getting along, or she would get a note from a doctor that would allow her to be on "bed rest" at DESC. Her son's lease did not allow her to stay there more than four days at a time and she hated staying at DESC during the day because of the noise, the smoke, and the general atmosphere. When she was able to, she would go to the Y in the morning to a therapeutic swim for which a doctor had given her a pass. After swimming she would need to find some place quiet to rest her back and this was difficult to do.

> That's another problem. I get done swimming and I need to go somewhere to rest. And I can't really do that. I can do that at the library.... the library is great. You see if I go to Angeline's it is full of people, all these places are full of people.... So I've been doing a lot walking after I've been swimming which I shouldn't. I should be resting.

When she did go down to her son's for a few days she liked to take him some food from the food bank, so some of her day to day life was made up of picking up cans of food and storing them in a locker that she rented by the month at the Y. She did this despite the fact that it was very hard for her to carry any weight at all. Whenever I saw Carla she had several nice bags or purses with her in which she carried the things that she would need during the day. She tried to walk everywhere she went since she knew that it was good exercise and good for her back, but she was clearly being challenged by her homeless lifestyle.

> You see that is another problem. I can't lift hardly anything. Like I want to go to the food bank. I have all this food stuck in my locker at the Y. It's food to take down to my son to try to save money. But that is how I hurt myself.... I can't lift anything.... I take little bits down to my son. I want to go to the food bank today and get some stuff, but how am I going to carry it?

Frieda and her "old man" had chronic lung conditions that became worse during the winter due to catching colds. They were living in their station wagon, in which she had been quite happy in the autumn, but which was proving to be too uncomfortable in the frigid temperatures.

> It's cold! I mean we have a lot of blankets. It is still not the same thing [as having a place to live]. He sleeps in the back of

the car because he has long legs, so he can stretch out. I sleep in the front seat. We can't even sleep in the back together.

When I asked her where they went during the day to rest and recuperate because they were both sick, she said:

> There is nowhere to go to relax. We go upstairs [DESC] or over to the Third Avenue Service Center. About the only places we've got to go. Can't really relax. . . . Oh you can lie down at either of them, but who wants to? I'd just as soon stay in the car.

Sometimes they both had such trouble breathing that it was hard to walk. Frieda used a wheel chair at these times and her boyfriend pushed her, despite his own condition.

> When I get a cold I get really bound up. The old man pushes me. . . . I could never push him. Sometimes I hear him huffing and puffing and I say "Take a break!".

Frieda and her "old man" lived on their combined incomes from her SSI check and his General Assistance check. Frieda supplemented this income with a small amount of hourly work at a business near where their car was parked. In addition, her boyfriend made trips to the plasma center to give blood when they needed extra money. Frieda couldn't do that any longer although she had gone regularly in the past.

> No, they have too much trouble finding my veins. I used to go. I've been going since 1975, but I had to give it up last year. It looks like tracks in that one area of my arms. That is from plasma.

Irene left a shelter situation where she did not have to pay rent or buy food in order to move into an SRO. Paying rent and part of the deposit the first month left her with very little money for food. At the end of the first month of living in the SRO she was needing to come to Angeline's for lunch on a daily basis and she made frequent trips to the food bank. Although she was diabetic and not able to do many kinds of work she thought about going to pick up some day labor in order to make ends meet. I think that she did not do this in the end partly because she started spending time with her ex-boyfriend again who would bring her food on the nights he came to see her.

Hilda worked hard to keep her spirits up even when her life was feeling a little gloomy. She tended to be particularly cheerful when she was in good contact with her family, when she was not drinking, and when she was employed. The times that were most difficult for her were when she felt discriminated against due to her age as she tried to secure work. But she never let her unemployment, her financial or living situation incapacitate her so that she couldn't get up the next day and try again. At the holidays she became impatient with the self pity manifested by some of the other residents where she was living:

> One woman always gets depressed. This is the one I was just talking to. She knew I was going to my family's. She said she might as well go to the morgue. I told her "This is Christmas. Try to relax!". She is so depressing. I said "If I couldn't get there [to her family's house] on the bus I wouldn't panic, I have my books, I have my knitting". I like to read anyway. If you don't have a back up you just sit around and feel sorry for yourself.... especially at the holiday. I can't get into their problems. It will just bring me down. I'm up again. I think you can tell. I'm back with my family. When I left Lutheran [LCC] because I was drinking, my daughter wouldn't talk to me. I'm not going to screw up again.... Some of these people are so depressing. "I'm probably going to die" [they say]. For goodness sake, grow up. I've never been suicidal. For goodness sake, you've been given a life, live it. It may not be the way you want to live it. Use it. That's all I can say.

On her return from her visit with her daughter at Christmas, Hilda planned to try again to find work. She was willing to take a cut in pay if it was necessary in order to have a steady job. She thought that maybe her resiliency was partly due to her age.

> Yes I am a lot older than a lot of these people. The one that is suicidal is 45, that is not exactly a kid. Another one who is shaking all the time is really young. Everyone has a problem.

> Mine is alcohol. It is never beaten. I just watch it. And as I say if they don't have a job on Wednesday then I will fill out my application for Pay and Save and I can try McDonald's. Even five dollars an hour is OK. I've heard that if they like you, you can be promoted.

When Angie decided to move back into her apartment and throw her abusive boyfriend out, she took matters into her own hands to make sure she was safe.

> I said "I want you out" and so he said he'd be gone by Saturday. So I came by on Thursday, and he wasn't here. I told the landlady I was there and I said "change the locks". She said she couldn't do it until Tuesday. So I said I would do it myself.

For four months Angie was successful in keeping her boyfriend out of her apartment. She had friends living with her partly in order to help them out, but also to help herself, as they provided company, safety and some financial assistance. Eventually her boyfriend did get into her apartment at which time he ransacked the apartment, verbally abused her friend, verbally abused Angie and broke a mirror over her head. She and her friend left that apartment and found a new place to live. She began drinking heavily again during this time and lost her job.

She was hopeful that the move to the new apartment would serve as a fresh start, and that she would be able to get her life together. She did temporary work for several weeks until she took a permanent job at lower wages than she was accustomed to. She and her roommate were having a hard time making ends meet when I last saw her. When I offered to take her out to dinner for our termination interview, she chose to go to Kentucky Fried Chicken so that we could buy a big bucket of chicken to take back to her apartment. Paying the bills was always a balancing act that took considerable ingenuity. When her work schedule allowed it she would go to the food bank, to save spending money on groceries. She had asked the Lion's Club to help her to get glasses since she didn't have insurance to cover that and had been without glasses for months. One month she told me how she had paid the bills:

> I paid the rent, paid the cable and sent an unsigned check to the phone company, so that gives me a little time. I could borrow money at work, but I don't want to. Or I could go down to the bar and write a check that they would hold.

Despite the hardships that she faced daily, Angie remains optimistic about her future and satisfied with life's small pleasures. She minimized the difficulties and was thankful for what she had: "I don't think any one ever said that you are supposed to be comfortable all the time. I've got a whole lot more than a whole lot of people."

NORMALCY

As in the last chapter on pathways to homelessness, the theme of normalcy emerges from the data in the area of day to day life. The women's accounts contradicted the myth of crazy bag women doing eccentric things with their lives. None of these women fit this stereotype all the time, and few of them did any of the time. As a way of presenting the data that manifest normality, I have chosen to describe one or two behaviors or activities, for each of the eleven women as evidence for this theme of normalcy.

Angie did her best to have a nice time at the holidays in order not to feel too lonely for her children who lived on the other side of the state. At Thanksgiving she and her friends cooked a big meal and she had 30 people over to her very small apartment for the feast. This was soon after she had moved back after two months in a shelter.

Beatrice had a ritual to her day that involved going over to the Federal Building for coffee and breakfast every morning. She would go there by herself or with friends to have a little social time away from her institutional living in the shelter.

> We've been coming in here for years. A lot of us from the shelter down there walk over here. We have our little breakfast, or our little coffee or whatever it is we are going to do. And then we go out and get back on the bus and go over to Angeline's and have a sandwich there and visit among us. Smoke and choke. Things you know.

Carla loved nature and was an artist. Part of the reason she went to her son's was in order to paint and store her paintings. She also was interested in writing and did write poetry and letters to politicians. She spent much of her free time reading. Like many Americans, she was concerned about her weight on an ongoing basis, and she knew that the food that was served at the shelters was high in fat and carbohydrates. When she could afford it she would skip the free food and buy yogurt and fresh fruits and vegetables for herself.

> When I asked Carla how she spent her time at her son's she said: I just watch television. He has a big color TV. I watch the Discovery channel. I watch all the animals. I love animals, do you? And then the second day I try to paint. I've got something in my head now that I want to get on canvas.

And when I asked her how she spent her time at the shelter she said:

> Sometimes I go to sleep right away. I usually have to lie down and I read. I'm studying Spanish again. I've got a really good book called *Direct Encounters* if you ever get the chance to get the book. It's all about extraterrestrial beings.

Dierdra remained in contact with her family by visiting them on occasion and spending some time with them at holidays. She has a payee for her SSI check so she didn't have a lot of freedom about how she spent that money. One time she was telling me all the things that she had done and wanted to do with her money. They all revolved around her family. She spoke of a party for her nine year old, developmentally disabled son:

> We had birthday cake and I went and bought balloons with what money I had. And they blew them up and I got some whistles.

She wished that she could buy him a Halloween costume:

> I'm not going to have enough money to get a costume for that little retarded boy either. . . . He said he wanted a costume. I don't know how I'm going to get it.

As she anticipated receiving $5 from me she thought of yet another thing she'd like to be able to buy:

> I want to go get some flowers to put on my mother's grave, but I'm not going to have enough money with that 5 dollars.

Before Elsie became involved with the boyfriend with whom she later rented an apartment, she had many male friends and admirers. One day when I went to find her at the shelter she was very sick and on "bed rest". She told me that she had something to show me and she took me back to the dark corner where she was sleeping. There in a vase of sorts were a dozen long-stemmed red roses that someone had sent her to cheer her up. She didn't know who they were from but they made her very happy and very curious.

Frieda was the only woman in my sample who did not have children. She did have three cats that shared her station wagon, and later a trailer, with her and her boyfriend. They called these cats "the kids" and treated them with a great deal of love. Sometimes they would go camping with the cats:

> .... Car cats, camper cats. When we go camping we let them out and let them run and they never go far from camp.

When I asked her where they would go to camp she said:

> Cascades, Mt. Rainier, anywhere, summer, winter...the freebies. I have the golden age pass, so we can pay half price for the ones you need to pay. I have a fishing license for the rest of my life.

Gayla talked about having more than one life and perhaps more than one personality. She was very uncomfortable with the status of being a homeless woman and worked hard to set herself apart from other homeless people. She spent much of her time outside of the downtown area--where she felt unsafe--applying for work, window shopping in the malls, visiting with her grandson. One of her favorite activities was being a clown in parades, something she has been doing for years.

Day to Day Lives

Gayla was a writer and had published a small book of proverbs. When I first met her she showed me what the cover of her second edition was going to look like.

> I was able to get these printed and they will be sold in a gift store in Auburn. I went to Bellingham to have it designed. Nordstrom's helped me find the materials for the cover. I need another $600 to get the rest of it done before Christmas.

She was unable to complete that project during data collection, though her identity as an author remained important to her.

Hilda had many hobbies to keep her busy when she was not working. She knit, she took walks around the neighborhood, she wrote letters to her children or talked with them on the phone, or she socialized with the other residents where she lived. Mostly she enjoyed her privacy and found pleasure in being by herself doing what she liked to do.

> Yesterday they were watching an absolutely dreadful movie. So I came in here, into the tranquil room and I turned on the TV and turned down the volume and listened to Christmas carols on the stereo...My idea of heaven is sitting in bed reading my book for a half an hour and eating my candy. My family says they'd much rather have me get fat then drinking. I've always had a sweet tooth. I'm not ashamed of it. I enjoy it.

Irene very consciously looked for things to do to occupy her time and thoughts so that she wouldn't be tempted to go to see her exboyfriend. She purposefully sought out people in order not to be lonely. She was involved in two different education and training programs while I knew her, which she enjoyed very much; she also enjoyed going to support groups and meeting with counselors. She was a part of a church community north of Seattle where she would occasionally go and where she found support from the pastor and the congregation. Her strategies to stay busy and involved were very normal ones for someone trying to stay out of an unhealthy relationship:

The last few days I've been telling myself I don't need to see my ex-boyfriend. There are other things I can do like go jogging, well I don't jog, but walking. Or go see people.

Perhaps of all the women in my sample, Jackie was the one that most closely fit the stereotype of a homeless bag woman. She would often meet me without shoes on and with a blanket wrapped around her shoulders. She carried her possessions in shopping bags. Most of the time that I knew Jackie, she did not have any money, as her SSDI check had not yet been transferred to Seattle from where she had last lived.

The last time we met together she did have some money left from the check she had gotten earlier in the month and she was very generous with it. When a small child came into the restaurant where we were meeting Jackie noticed that the child wanted a bag of chips. When the child's mother told her to put them back, Jackie offered to buy them for the child. She also offered a cigarette to one of the women that worked at the restaurant from whom she thought she had bummed a cigarette in the past.

Katy was living at a shelter downtown when I met with her. She did not enjoy the downtown area and preferred to be in the northern suburbs where she used to live. She would often take a bus up north during the day in order to be in an area that was more familiar to her. One thing that she liked to do when she had the money was to go to a hotel she knew of and use their swimming pool and jacuzzi. She also liked to go shopping with her 16 year old daughter and generally spent part of her SSDI check each month buying outfits for her daughter.

The normalcy theme emphasizes that beyond the circumstance of being without a home, these women led lives and did things that are not unlike many other women in our society. It serves to challenge the notion that homeless people are somehow different from the mainstream.

POLITICAL AWARENESS

The final theme to be presented in this chapter on day to day living is that of political awareness. Several of the women showed considerable assertiveness and political savvy in dealing with slum lords and lecherous managers. Others were instrumental in starting petitions and letter writing campaigns in order to let city officials know their views. I will give a few examples of this political astuteness in this chapter and present more in the next, where I will report on the women's visions for the future.

As mentioned in the last chapter Frieda and her "old man" stopped paying rent when they felt that their landlord was not meeting his end of the bargain. Their case went to court and they won in that the judge agreed the that apartment was substandard and that the landlord could not ask them to pay for repairs; they still needed to leave the apartment for nonpayment of rent. Angie also had a case out against her landlady for the months of inconvenience to her while her landlady did renovations. She eventually settled out of court and was given a rent reduction. She was threatening to take her landlady to court again due to negligence on apartment repairs when her boyfriend ransacked her apartment; she decided it was wiser to just move out of the building.

Beatrice claimed that she had had many bad experiences when she had stayed in SRO's and subsidized apartments. She felt that she had been unfairly discriminated against:

> Once you move into an apartment and the landlord knows that you have been homeless, they can't seem to keep their trap shut and the word is suddenly out. And people, rather than getting to know you, I think that there is something that is missing between their brain and their mouth and they have verbal diarrhea and they spread the word all over the building. Therefore I have found that people kind of look at you funny and everything that goes wrong in that apartment building is blamed on you and yours.

She told of one particularly distressing experience and how she handled it:

> This one place where I moved in the landlord used his own key, comes into the bedroom and ejaculates on your bedclothes and then leaves. Now I heard this about him almost immediately after moving in, and I really thought to myself, "Oh you pigs, is that all you can do is sit around and...yuck" and I pay no attention. And I am sitting on the bedroom floor one evening reading *Gone with the Wind*. I hear someone

> knock at the door. And they tap again. I'm not opening my mouth and I'm not opening the door. Finally I see the handle turn and I hear a key in the lock and the door opens and I say "To what do I owe this honor?" He said that he was looking for prowlers.

To make matters worse the tub didn't work and she had no shades.

> And they wouldn't fix the shades and right across the way from me there was an old man who was so fat and bald and all he did was watch TV all night long, and there was no way I could open the windows. . . . When I told him [the landlord] the bathtub didn't work he said "Not to worry just come around the corner, you can take a bath in my apartment any time you want." I said "Gee thanks, but no thanks." He said, "I don't know where you'll take a shower, you'll get kind of gamey." I said "No, it is nice weather, I'll walk down to Angeline's and have my shower and wash my hair there." And he said "What about winter?" And I said "Well that is the question, will you have the tub fixed by winter?"

Beatrice eventually stopped paying the rent and the landlord called the police on her.

> So when the policemen came I said, "I am very happy to see you and while you are here, do you mind stepping into the bathroom and see that the tub doesn't drain and there are no shades, and I have cataracts and can't fix them." The policemen looked at the tub and then looked at the shades and mentioned to me that it is a misdemeanor if I didn't pay my rent on time and I mentioned back to them that it had to be a misdemeanor for them to ask for rent when the apartment was unlivable. I said that I planned to do every thing I could to make sure it was a misdemeanor. So we went around and around. And finally they said I had four days to get out. They didn't want to get involved.

Not surprisingly, Beatrice preferred living at the shelter, where at least she didn't have to pay rent for dismal living conditions.

During the data collection period there was collective action by a group of homeless individuals in the Seattle area. A tent city was formed in protest to the lack of shelter space in the city. I asked Carla if she was at all involved in the action.

> I thought about getting involved with them.... but the thing about it too.... is that if you are a woman and alone.... I don't know I don't want to put myself in any position where people might take advantage of me.... It is all run by guys and I don't trust men. After all the stuff I've been through why would I?

In the end she did spend a few nights at the tent city until it was too difficult for her to be there because of her back.

One result of the tent city action was the opening of a temporary winter shelter for adult women. Carla was very pleased with this shelter and felt it was a great improvement over where she had been staying previously. She organized taking a petition over to the mayor's office requesting that the shelter stay open all year. She got 68 signatures from women at the shelter, women on the streets, and some men and women from the senior center. She also helped to organize a group of women to write thank you cards to the mayor letting him know that they appreciated the shelter.

Near the end of the data collection period I learned that a group of people had started a "Homeless Newspaper". Carla and Gayla both became actively involved in this venture and were able to use this medium as an outlet for both their writing talents and their political views on oppression.

The four themes of relationships, resiliency, normalcy and political awareness were evident in the present, daily lives of these homeless and near-homeless women just as they had been in the stories women told of their past, and how it was that they came to be homeless. These four themes also emerged from the women's description of their hopes and plans for the future, presented in the next chapter.

CHAPTER 6

PLANS AND HOPES FOR THE FUTURE

INTRODUCTION

This chapter discusses both the women's hopes and plans for the future for themselves personally, and for homeless women in general. I did not often ask the women directly about their future plans, other than in the area of housing. Nevertheless I learned, over the data collection time period, about some of their dreams and aspirations. Again the themes of relationships, resiliency, normalcy and political awareness provide the framework for presenting the women's plans and desires for the future.

RELATIONSHIPS

As the last two chapters have shown, the women in my sample did not lead isolated lives separated from human contact and loving relationships. Admittedly, many of their intimate relationships, both with lovers and children, were problematic, and these women had hopes for closer ties in the future with their children and for love relationships that were less abusive than what they had known in the past.

Angie's two teenage children lived with her former husband's parents in a town several hundred miles away. Although she felt that they were better off there than with her, she missed them tremendously and would have liked to have been able to spend more time with them, if not to actually live with them. At our first interview she said:

> That's part of the reason I'm trying to make a change now. When my daughter turns 15 she may want to be where I am. That's part of the reason I left R. [boyfriend] this last time. She [daughter] said "Why do you let him do that to you? You wouldn't let anyone do that to me." She's real wise.

Her daughter turned 15 during data collection; Angie talked about going to see her for the birthday, but money was short, so she comforted herself by saying that the 16th birthday would be more important anyway. Before she lost her job she had thought she'd be able to have her children come to visit her during the summer, given that she no longer lived with her abusive boyfriend, and was not drinking. By the end of data collection, she had lost the job, was drinking and was in less frequent contact with her children. She was less likely to call them and write to them when her life was unstable.

While I knew Angie, she was actively trying to stay free of a particular abusive relationship. This was difficult for her. "I'd like to see us together and happy for the rest of our lives. I don't see that as workable." Most of the men she knew she met in bars, and she knew those relationships were not going to be healthy ones either. She said that she would like a different type of relationship. She was not sure if she, or the men that she met, really knew how to date or if dating was just some romantic notion she had gotten from TV. She spoke of how she would like one man, who was pursuing her when I knew her, to behave: "If he wants to take me out to dinner, I'm happy to go out to dinner with him--if he wants to court me and woo me." At our last interview she talked about wanting to be with her ex-boyfriend again merely for sex. She had a fear of AIDS and she knew he was safe. She talked about wanting to rent a man for an hour and that she had even bought a bunch of condoms in preparation for that.

Carla was out of communication with her daughter at the time of data collection. She hoped that in time that they would be able to talk again, once her daughter had a chance to grow up. (She did reconnect with her daughter after data collection was complete; see previous chapter.) Relations with her son were also up and down which she attributed to his self-centeredness and immaturity.

> I told my daughter "I will help you as much as I can to go to school." I told her that she was young, beautiful and smart. I

Plans and Hopes for the Future

told her "Stop spending time with that guy who is no good for you.".... I don't need to be hurt by her. I have my own problems. With my son it would be fine if he would listen to what I want, too, but he doesn't. So I need to think about staying away from that. I don't need that. It is hard to live with your children after a certain age. I asked my daughter once if she could think of me as a person. And she said that she couldn't, she could only think of me as her mother. That is when you need to get away and let them grow up.

When things were going well with her son, Carla did consider trying to live with him. Although getting an apartment for herself was her first choice, she knew living with her son for a while might be an option. One concern she had about moving in with her son was that he would find a girlfriend and then she would be in the way. Only once did Carla mention the possibility of getting involved with a man again, and it was in context of the possibility of living with her son.

If I came home with Burt Reynolds, it wouldn't be good enough for him [her son]. Isn't that cute? I'm lucky to have him. He's talking about buying a house.... He said I could come live with him but then if he meets someone then I'd be in the way. But maybe for a while, while I get my life together.... He thinks that having me around might make him more stable.... I'll play it as it goes. I'll just try to save money. I've found that you can't really plan things. He might meet someone tomorrow. I wouldn't mind meeting someone again myself.

Throughout data collection, Dierdra was waiting to get into subsidized housing. Supposedly her caseworker was working out the arrangements. She mentioned various different places she was waiting to hear from over the months. Her youngest child was living with her aunt. I believe her older child was living independently. At times Dierdra would talk about having her own place so that her children could come live with her, but I am not sure any of the places she was considering would allow her to have her children with her, nor am I sure she would get custody of her youngest child given her developmental disability. All the same, at least some of the time, her dream of having her own place to live included having her son with her.

At every one of our interviews, Elsie spoke of her three daughters who lived in the Southwest. Because Elsie was prone to exaggeration and story telling, it was hard to know whether to believe any of her plans for seeing her daughters. For example, at one time during data collection she had said she was going to Arizona, where they lived, the following week in order to participate in a custody trial concerning her "baby" girl--whom she wanted back. Supposedly her oldest daughter, who was married and with a baby of her own, was trying to get custody of Elsie's youngest daughter. In the end, Elsie did not go to Arizona and I'm not sure the custody battle ever existed. This was one of many of her planned trips that did not happen.

Elsie blamed her sister and brother-in-law for sexually abusing her youngest daughter once when she had left her in their custody, and she often spoke of getting even with this sister--that she had "business to take care of". Elsie was always talking about taking one trip or another, and the trip that she spoke of the most often was going to see her children. But she also seemed to not want to intrude on their lives and she would say "They know how to find me if they need me." Even when she had her own apartment and telephone she did not call them, although she said that she did write to them to let them know where she was. At our last interview when I asked her if she was lonely, she said no, although she missed her daughters and wished that they would write to her. She clearly missed them and would have liked them to be more a part of her life. When I first met Elsie and asked her if she wrote to her daughters she said:

> No I just go to see them when they send for me. Hopefully they'll come to see me. I want them to live with me. I need a five bedroom house.

At my last interview with Elsie she had been with her boyfriend for over four months. This was longer than she stayed with three of her four husbands. Although she had mixed feelings about this relationship, she generally seemed happy with it. She said that now that she was the payee for his SSDI check she would have to stay with him. I asked her if she felt trapped and she said yes, but that she knew she could get out of it any time she wanted to. Whenever she spoke of

Plans and Hopes for the Future

future plans they included her boyfriend. Despite the fact that at the end of data collection she was spending almost all of her time with her boyfriend and no one else, Elsie maintained her independence. When I asked her if she missed her old friends from the shelter she said:

> I don't want to associate with them. They are panhandlers and such. C. [her boyfriend] feels that way too. C. says that the only true friend he has is me.... My only true friend is myself.

Gayla was in contact with her children to some degree during data collection. She babysat her grandson for her daughter twice a month, and did get together with all her five children on Thanksgiving. They did not know that she lived in a shelter as she didn't want to embarrass them or make them feel responsible. In fact she had thought about making the Thanksgiving dinner a sort of farewell dinner in order to slip quietly out of their lives.

Her children frequently hurt her feelings. For example, at the Thanksgiving dinner they talked about her ex-husband and his new wife and about the Christmas they would be having with them:

> At first they just sat there at my expense, not just emotionally but financially. But my daughter didn't know I was paying for it. But I didn't want to come in the rain to hear about her step mother needing $10,000 to have dental work done. Yeah my husband's wife. When she is inheriting all my kid's money.... And they kept talking about what they were going to get them for Christmas, while I was going to have an un-Christmas.

When she made her speech about it being a farewell dinner one of her daughter's said, "Oh Mom, there you go again always saying that."

Gayla felt very torn about her children. Despite the farewell at Thanksgiving she did attempt to stay in contact with them for as long I knew her. While she loved them and was proud of them, she was unsure that she meant as much to them as they did to her. This depressed her and affected her plans for the future. She recited to me something she had written one day after we had been talking about a bad incident with one of her children: "I am but a vapor in the wind, being carried off into a vacuum of nothingness, nonexistent to all the loved ones I have touched."

Gayla thought that she got along best with children, and now that her own children were grown they no longer understood her.

> You know something that I've found with my kids is that children love me the most and teenagers. I really have good rapport with teenagers too. In fact when I was looking to get my foster parent license again I was hoping to have a teenage boy.

My sense is that despite the hurt she sometimes felt from her children that Gayla would continue to stay in contact with them. In fact, since the end of data collection I have received one phone call from her inviting me to go with her to a wedding of one of her daughters so that I could see her in a "normal" environment. She was nervous about the event and what might take place given the people that would be there.

Hilda openly grieved for her ex-boyfriend in our first interview. She talked of him less as the months passed but she often mentioned waiting for "Mister Right". She said that she would love to meet someone with a million dollars who would expect her to stay home rather than go out and work. She said that she had old fashioned romantic ideas.

> It is not that I have never known love. After all I've been married two times and lived with another man eight years.... But I would like to come home to someone or have someone come home to me. But I will take things as they come... one day at a time.

Irene was trying hard during the data collection period to reestablish connections with her children with whom she had been separated for years. She spent considerable time writing them letters, thinking about them and talking about them. She said that she wasn't close to her own family when she was growing up and she'd like for it to be different with her children. Being close to her children seemed like a priority in Irene's life. At our termination interview, she had plans to go to Oregon in order to see her son in prison and to meet with her daughter whom she'd not seen for 20 years.

Plans and Hopes for the Future

Another priority in Irene's life was to stay away from her ex-boyfriend who had been abusive to her. This was very difficult for her to do and she did allow him to stay with her at her SRO for a few weeks during data collection when he had no place to live. She said that she had felt sorry for him and she was lonely. He was the only man that she had spent time with for years, although now she was trying to build up a support system and to fill her time with other activities. Irene went to see a counselor on a weekly basis primarily to improve her self-esteem and to help her shape a future life for herself which included healthy relationships.

Both Jackie and Katy wished that they were living with their respective daughters. Jackie's daughter was grown and with a family of her own and did not want Jackie intruding on her life. Jackie had dealt with this by traveling and keeping herself from being too isolated.

> I don't miss my family because I am around other people. But if you are by yourself, then all you have to think about is your family.

In the short time that I knew Jackie she talked about wanting to go back to New York state to see her daughter, and did in fact make one aborted trip while I knew her. She spent all her money in Montana and didn't reach New York. The trips she had taken back to New York in the past sounded as though they had been frustrating with unwanted hospitalizations and lack of support from her brothers and daughter. All the same, her daughter remained central in Jackie's thoughts and conversations, and plans for the future.

Katy's life also seemed to revolve around her daughter who was in foster care. Katy's primary hope for the future was to get an apartment large enough for herself, her daughter and her daughter's baby to be. Katy felt that many people and the system were out to get her--trying to prevent her from having this domestic life that she wanted. She planned to fight to have her family back together again in a house of their own.

Perhaps not all these future hopes and plans are realistic. Some of the women may not be able to live independently with their children because of a mental or developmental disability. Finding a "Mister Right" who is financially independent, healthy and caring is quite unlikely for most middle-aged women--probably even more so for homeless, middle-aged women. But the dreams of better relationships with loved ones in the future appeared to help the women deal with the day to day hardships and disappointments.

RESILIENCY

The mere fact that all these women kept on hoping and dreaming for a better future than what they were experiencing in their present lives, despite the barriers they faced daily is evidence of their resiliency. Their good humor as they met each new obstacle manifested itself in their plans for their future lives.

Beatrice had been living at DESC on and off for years. She had spent some time in subsidized housing and SRO's, but generally she had not had good experiences at these places. She had decided that the best way for her to get an apartment that suited her tastes was to learn how to manage an apartment building herself. She had decided to take classes to learn how to do this.

> I have made an arrangement with the YWCA where I'll go to school to learn to take over an apartment house. Now I've had a lot of experience in this particular type of work. I need help and I need the theory [sic] to rent the place. But for right now people are going to take anything that they can get. But for future reference, I would like to have that under my belt, so I can discuss leases and such with future tenants.

Frieda and her boyfriend were becoming very sick during the cold winter months and their doctors were trying to get them subsidized housing so that they would not have to live in their car. The housing office put them off and told them it would be weeks before they could have an appointment to talk with someone about getting an apartment. So they decided to take matters into their own hands and they started looking for a trailer. Because they would not have the money to make payments on a trailer and also pay for a lot on which to park the trailer, Frieda decided to ask local businesses near where she had a small part-time job if she could park outside their building and use their electricity.

> We're thinking about putting it down right where we're at, or if I can get down to some of these businesses down where

Plans and Hopes for the Future 95

> we're at, and see if I can hook up for electric. It is rigged for electric. It doesn't have a bathroom, but I could get a portapotty of some sort. That will work...What I'd like to do is maybe find some place by one of the buildings and hook up to their electrical and water and pay them so much a month. We'd have our electrical and our water and we wouldn't have any worries there.

When I last saw Frieda she hadn't talked with any businesses yet, mostly because the business across the street from where they first parked their trailer called the city and they eventually had to move. I lost track of Frieda after that. (I heard from her one year later by mail. Her partner had taken ill and died during data collection.)

Throughout the time that I knew her, Gayla was trying to find work. She felt caught between her desire to be financially independent, through employment, and her need to maintain her SSDI check until she could be financially independent. She was angry that the welfare system ultimately discouraged people from working. At our last interview she seemed to have come to some sort of resolution on this issue so that she could get an apartment and have some security. She decided that she would try to get a Section 8 apartment given her disability status--with which she disagreed--continue to get her disability check, and begin to put more time and effort into her writing. She would be able to make up to $100 each month on her book without jeopardizing her SSDI check. Although she hated to be labeled as mentally disabled, she had decided to try to make the system work for her so that she could begin to work more consistently on her writing, and have a place to live.

At another interview, Gayla articulated this theme of resiliency in one of her proverbs that she wrote: "When you hit rock bottom, you push yourself up with both feet or you'll be lost forever in quick sand." She talked about needing to be a fighter in order to survive. She had spent most of her life being sweet and kind, and now she knew she needed to be harsher at times.

> I can't be sweet all the time anymore. Gayla is still sweet. It is the other people in me that are the fighters. The writer, the entertainer, the crude sayer. . . . I call myself the crude sayer. I'd like to have a newspaper called that: the Crude Sayer.

Irene, at 57, was trying to get her GED. She said that she had never thought she would go back to school. When I first met her she had been taking morning GED classes three days a week for about six months-- since she had most recently left her boyfriend. During the data collection period she began another program that had classes daily. This program was also going to help her with basic education skills and eventually give her some job training. It was an eight week long program. She planned to keep up her studying for her GED while in this program and then return to those classes after the eight week program concluded. Both the GED and the employment training programs were governmentally funded programs, targeting older, impoverished individuals. After spending most of her life on public assistance or doing low-wage work she said that she was excited to think that maybe she could go on to try to get some training with "business computers or something" after she got her GED. She thought that might be "kind of fun". Irene was really trying hard to improve her life despite the difficulties she faced daily. She hoped for a future that included things she had not known in the past: an education, a good job, good relationships with her children, and a solid self-esteem that allowed her to stay free of abusive relationships.

Hilda had left most of her belongings in storage in California when she moved up to the Seattle area. She tried to keep up on the payments for that storage, but it eventually became too much for her and she lost all of her belongings, except the few things she had given to her children to store for her. When she learned that the storage facility would not keep her belongings any longer unless she paid up her bill, she wrote to them and asked them at least to send her her family pictures; they did this.

During the time that I knew Hilda, she seemed to be biding her time until she could get an apartment of her own so that she could move out of the community living situation she was in. She thought that a very small apartment would be fine and the fact that her children had a few of her pieces of furniture and the sentimental things about which she cared most, allowed her to be very courageous about losing so many of her possessions. Although she was having a very difficult time paying the low rent at the transitional housing center where she lived, much less, save any money for her upcoming move, she remained optimistic that she would be able to move by Autumn. She

Plans and Hopes for the Future

resiliently kept working at any job she could in order to keep her bills paid so that she could hang onto a hope for a better future.

Throughout the time that I knew Carla she often spoke of various places she might like to move where she might be able to find a better life than what she was living in Seattle. She thought these other places might offer better job opportunities, more sun, better doctors, better shelters, or an easier time getting SSI. By our last interview she was feeling more hopeful about staying in Seattle despite the hard time she had had all winter. She had recently learned that her General Assistance eligibility had been extended for another 6 months which gave her the security she needed to be able to think about applying for subsidized housing. She thought maybe she could deal with the gloomy weather by trying to get out to the Olympic Peninsula every once in a while for some fresh air and some time in nature. Also she was beginning to get excited about some of the new projects in which she was getting involved, like the homeless newspaper. So in the characteristically hopeful manner that all these women portrayed, she said that she was going to try to be thankful for what she had going. She thought things might be better now that spring had arrived. (Carla did in fact get a subsidized apartment in a Seattle suburb soon after data collection was completed.)

In the last two months that I knew Angie she lost her job and had to move to a new apartment. She immediately started to work at temporary jobs after settling into her new place. Within a couple weeks she took a permanent, full-time job at very low wages. It was difficult for her to pay her bills with this income and the job was boring for her. Despite the long hours that she put in at the job she was also applying for other jobs and going to interviews. She tried not be discouraged about her future and said "By the time I'm fifty something will happen. I used to say by the time I'm forty, but now I have to say by the time I'm fifty."

At this last interview I learned that Angie and her roommate did not have enough money for food and that they had already received a late notice for the second month's rent at their new apartment. When I asked her if she was worried about that. She said, "No, if I worried about everything I would have ulcers." With a sense of humor that seemed to allow her to meet her daily challenges, she spoke of her less than successful attempts to find another job, to stay away from her ex-boyfriend, and to stay sober and healthy. She was hopeful about the future and thankful for her wonderful support system of friends. Several days after this last interview she sent me a lovely card thanking me for being one of those friends that helped her to keep going.

NORMALCY

The dreams these women had for their futures were very normal dreams. They were hopes for an existence better than what they had, yet their aspirations tended to be quite humble. Not surprisingly most of them wanted their own homes, a little privacy, to have good relationships with their children, to be safe, and to be treated with self respect.

Angie even articulated her dreams for the future as dreams for a "normal life". Once she was telling me about the sort of relationship and lifestyle she longed for:

> I'd just like a normal person who can accept me for what I am. Just be normal, go to work and come home. I really liked that with my ex-husband. I use to do tupperware parties and drink coffee with neighbors. I liked that.

Carla had been living in shelters for a couple of years. She would have loved to work, but problems with her back had prevented her from being employed at the telephone work which she had done in the past because she became immobilized in pain after just a few days of sitting. She would have loved to have a part-time job doing something that interested her.

> So I guess all I can do is swim and take advantage of whatever programs and just hope that I do get well enough. Maybe sell some artwork, maybe go back to school. I'd love to have a real job. A job that I had something worthwhile to give it. I have to be.... not inspired.... what is the word.... I have to be "pumped".... maybe I could work part-time counseling and feel good about what I was doing and even do my artwork too. That would be the perfect type setup.

Plans and Hopes for the Future

Her ideal living situation would be to get a small subsidized apartment in the downtown area so that she could continue to walk to the various places where she spent time. She wanted to have a window with a view, a little space to do her artwork, and a cat.

From the first time that I met Elsie, when she was living downtown in a shelter, she was talking about living outside of the downtown area. At first she talked about getting a place up near the University so that she could go back to school and learn to be a psychologist. Within a month she had become involved with a man and moved with him to an apartment north of the downtown area. While I knew her she moved two more times, each time to a nicer place. I did not see the last place to which she moved, but she told me that it even had a little yard--something that was important to her. At our last interview she mentioned that once her boyfriend got the large check that the government owed him for which they were waiting, that they might buy a trailer and move out of the city all together. She still talked about going back to school. (Elsie and her boyfriend eventually moved to Oklahoma to live near her boyfriend's mother. She wrote to me frequently in the year after data collection.)

Katy and Gayla also both hated living in the downtown area. Katy was used to living in a northern suburb and having a yard with a garden she could work in. What she really wanted was an acre in the country where she could build her own home. Gayla wanted to find a section 8 apartment out of the downtown area; she always felt unsafe downtown. Eight years ago Gayla had lived in a large home in an upper-middle class suburb. She continued to pay $170 a month to store her antiques. She wanted to be able to have her own place and to have her things around her. She said many homeless people keep precious things in storage.

> You'd be surprised how many homeless people do that. They want to hold on to something in the hopes that life will be better. It allows for some hope.

When I last saw Frieda, she and her boyfriend were having to figure out where to move their trailer. All of their monthly income was being used up to make payments on the trailer so they didn't have any money left to pay for a trailer lot. Frieda had learned about a trailer park south of the city that sounded perfect to her if they could only afford it.

If we could afford it, which we can't right now, until we get everything paid off. There is a place I called about--a trailer park. I talked with the guy, he is an elderly gentleman. He said that he had a space available for $189 a month. That is the cheapest trailer park place I've ever heard of.... I don't know if we can do it or not, but in January I might try to get out to that trailer park out on Rainier. It would totally break us, but it would be worth it, at least we'd have a permanent place. It would cost us $289 to move in.

Hilda was really looking forward to being able to live on her own again soon. She was tolerating community living but she really preferred her privacy and having more control over her life. For example she found it difficult to cook in the community kitchen where she lived because other residents were messy and they stole food. So her hope was to be able to save enough money over the following six months in order to be able to rent a small apartment before the Christmas holidays. Although she had lost most of her possessions there were many things of both sentimental and practical value that she looked forward to having with her again once she had her own place.

My daughter and son-in-law have my swivel rocker and all my knitting needles and patterns which are very important to me, my work box which has all my cottons and stuff and my work basket. All my important stuff. And my dresser and my lamp. So I have most of the stuff I need anyway. My son has my TV and VCR and my daughter has my microwave and I might end up letting her keep that anyway. I can get a small one.

Dierdra wanted to get a place of her own. Throughout the time I knew her she would talk about one subsidized apartment building or another from which she was waiting to hear whether she could get in. After visiting one of these places she told me how she would be able to have cable TV if she moved in there, something she was quite excited about.

> They've got that TV stuff and they gave him money so that he could take care of his apartment--so he could have it in his apartment. All those switches that come from other countries. He can watch it all night, on channel 2.

Dierdra's mother had recently died and this had affected her deeply. She said that she wanted to have her own place soon before she got too old. "I'm just running around trying to find a place now so I can cool down before I get as old as my mother was." She also had hopes of having her children live with her again. Although I'm not sure if this was a realistic desire given her developmental disability, it certainly was a normal one. "I want to get my kids back. My sister wants me to hurry up and get a house." She once told me what she would do when she had her own place.

> My caseworker said that when I move I can have more food stamps. But I'm not going to have every Dick and Harry up there. Maybe Beatrice can come. We can talk and watch TV.

Beatrice, Dierdra, and I were together at this interview, and in that same conversation, Beatrice talked about what she would do when she got her own place. She talked about needing to go through all her possessions that she has stored in mini-storage.

> I still have all that stuff. But the next apartment that I get I will spend four or five days going through all that garbage and figuring out what I need and move with that. I'll keep the rest in mini storage. I have all the bills paid off now and that is great. . . . I want an apartment where I can afford the rent and buy my groceries. I have a little account at the Bon Marche.

I never got a very good sense of what Jackie would like for her future. When I first met her she said that she was trying to get a passport so that she could go to Europe. At our last interview I asked her if she was still planning to go to Europe and she said no, that she was American and that a lot of changes needed to happen here first. When I asked her what she would like to see changed, she said that she wanted to see her daughter become president. Again, this is perhaps not a realistic hope for the future but it is a fairly normal desire for a mother to have for a daughter whom she loves and admires.

That housing was a primary hope for the future for most of these homeless women is very normal, but given the current housing crisis, their hopes may not be realistic. On the one hand, three of the women did secure the apartments they wanted soon after data collection ended. Elsie moved to an apartment with a yard in a nice neighborhood, Irene got a subsidized apartment that was larger and cheaper than her SRO room, and Carla secured a subsidized apartment in a neighborhood west of the downtown area. On the other hand, two of the women who were eligible for subsidized housing due to their psychiatric disabilities, did not want to stay in the downtown area because it felt unsafe to them. Finding subsidized housing in the neighborhoods they liked would probably be very difficult.

It is possible that plans and hopes for the future voiced by some of the women, while normal enough, may be unrealistic given their psychiatric disabilities. I did not try to diagnose--nor could I--any of the women, but it is likely that mental health issues will sabotage the efforts of some of these women as they try to reach their goals and dreams.

POLITICAL AWARENESS

This last section of plans and hopes for the future presents some of the women's views about homelessness, discrimination, and inequality and how they see these factors affecting their future lives.

Carla and I talked about politics all the time. Although she had not completed high school, she was quite politically astute. During data collection, the United States was involved in the Gulf War. This made Carla very angry and for several months it was something that we talked about a lot. For example she often wondered how our president could be against abortion and for war. She was angry that tax dollars went for missiles rather than housing or other social services. At our last interview she read me a poem she had written called the "Power Structure":

Those filthy murdering bastards
With weapons so great

Plans and Hopes for the Future

> They cry for forgiveness
> But it will be too late.
> They are killing everything
> Precious and dear
> They ruin the nations
> With cruelty and fear.
> They will be undone
> Weapons and all
> For God will destroy them
> One by one.
> That's all.

Carla called herself a socialist. She said that she had read Marx and Lenin when she was just 12 or 13. She thought that Sweden had the best society because people were assured housing and income. She said to me on many occasions that she was not materialistic and that there were some parts of her simple homeless life that she thought were preferable to the stressful lives most people in our country lead.

> I think capitalism perpetuates greed. What are you competing for but material things. If you are just competing for the joy it would be different. But in our country they just hold up the Yankee dollar or something you can buy.... I am not materialistic. I figured out five or six years ago that money does not motivate me. It took me a long time to realize why I wasn't motivated. It just doesn't motivate me. I don't need a house in a wealthy suburb. I just need a small place with a lot of light where I could paint and have a cat.... I like living simply and not owing money. I don't want to buy things and owe money and be under stress.... That is why people are so unhappy. They don't have time for themselves. If I get a place for myself I might not even get a TV.

Carla was very concerned about the state of the environment. She even spent a portion of her small General Assistance check one month to buy an acre of land in the Brazilian rain forest because she thought that might be helpful in protecting it. One day she told me that she had been doing some writing about homelessness and that she had decided that as long as we had a planet there could be no homelessness. A couple months later she developed some of these thoughts into a poem which she shared with me.

>Homeless, I think not,
>Homeless I've been called, but I disagree
>How can I be homeless
>Or you, or we?
>For this mother planet is called mother earth
>It is home for you and home for me.
>For our species evolved here over millions of years
>And it is thought to survive.
>God created the earth,
>The stars and the sky.
>We are made to live here
>Each having a girl and a boy.
>Homeless I think not
>For how can they own the land, the sun, or the sky?
>But in the years to come
>God's wrath will be swept and their greed will be undone.
>God created the water and the earth and the sky.
>Homeless we're not
>It's just a big lie.
>For this is our birth place
>Our planet, you and I,
>And all the creatures
>They will prevail
>For God won't forsake them
>He has too much love to give.
>Homeless I think not
>It's just a big lie.
>This planet earth is our place
>To live and to die.
>This cradle of life
>So endless, so great,
>So rejoice my friends
>God will take charge
>Just wait and see.
>Homeless I think not
>Not you and not me.

Plans and Hopes for the Future

Elsie had a less defined philosophy of life than did Carla, but nonetheless she had one. While Carla may have used her creed of simple living to help her get through some of the harder times, Elsie clung to freedom. Often when I would ask her if she had done a certain thing or gone a certain place, she would let me know that she could do whatever she wanted and go anywhere she wanted whenever she wanted. Nothing was stopping her.

> I go everywhere. I go wherever I want to go. I am free and over twenty-one. I don't go just one place, I go around.

She was on SSI and had been for many years and all of her medical expenses were paid by Medicaid. She talked about the state taking care of everything which was the way she liked it.

> I don't have to pay for anything. Washington pays for me. I just sit back and relax and watch TV all day if I want to...Yeah the state pays for everything. They have to pay for my dental care and my medical care.

Although she was disabled and living on a very small income, Elsie never spoke of being discriminated against or of life being difficult. Her attitude was more that people always treated her like a princess, everything was going her way, and she could do whatever she wanted.

Beatrice had been to Washington DC the year before I knew her to testify in front of Congress on homelessness. She thought that politicians and people in general did not understand about homelessness and that they were ignoring the problem.

> Mr. W. [a local politician] doesn't understand this, he has never been homeless and it makes me think why the hell bother with the city council. They don't know anything. It is not one of their priorities any way. Their priorities are building up the water front, putting a garage in the convention center. To hell with the people who are homeless, that need a place. And I am thinking of those with children. Let the children sleep in the streets. They don't know how dangerous, cold and miserable it is for a child to have to be in the streets. And I'm not kidding. It makes me so mad, not angry, mad.

> And they don't think they've got a problem. . . . Do they want us to go out and put bricks through all the windows? I can think of about 50 or 60 things to do to really shake them up. I believe in sitting down and talking things over. I believe in me saying this is what I intend to do and you tell me what you intend to do and then we do it.

Gayla was very aware of being discriminated against because of her former mental illness, and felt that it plagued her every where she went.

> I was proud of my recovery. But you are not allowed to be proud. It is not like being a cancer patient. You're not allowed to be proud. . . . People have so much fear of mental illness. If you went out on the street and picked someone and asked them what do you have more fear of: having AIDS and dying in four years or being mentally ill and confined to hospitals for the next 20 years. Most people would rather die. . . . even though most people have never been in a hospital.

Sometimes she would say that discrimination due to poverty and homelessness was even worse.

> You have no credibility when you are poor. . . . when you are homeless there is more discrimination than ever from my former illness, you have no credibility on earth. You have never done anything in your life and you end up homeless. Anything you have done will go against you, and they don't like you.

Although I only met with Katy one time, it was clear in that one interview that she felt as though she had been treated unfairly by society. She was angry that she had lost her subsidized apartment which she had had for 18 years. She could not understand why she, who had not hurt anyone, should lose her home, when people that she knew dealt drugs still had theirs.

There ought to be a law that says that people that are disabled should be taken care of. Homes should not be taken away from disabled people.

All the eleven women were quite aware of the oppression they experienced as poor women in this society. Five of the women were analytical and verbal, not only about how their own present and future lives, but also about how society as a whole was worse off due to current inequities. They knew that this oppression would continue in the future unless these inequities were balanced out.

This last theme of political awareness relates to the final chapter of the findings which discusses services to homeless women. All of the women had something to say about the services which they received. In Chapter 7, their views about services for homeless women and their visions for future programs will be contrasted with those of the service providers whom I interviewed.

CHAPTER 7

SERVICES FOR HOMELESS WOMEN

INTRODUCTION

In this chapter I begin by discussing some of the specific things that women had to say about services which they had received, and about shelters they had stayed in, as homeless women. The women did not all agree. Some of their reflections were positive and some were negative. In the second section of the chapter I contrast their perceptions with the views of service providers.

WHAT THE WOMEN SAID

Use and Opinions of Shelters and Drop-In Center

Mid-way through data collection a shelter was opened up which was solely for single homeless women. Though it took some of the women in the sample a while to feel comfortable about leaving the shelter they had been staying at, those that did generally felt happy about the move. This shelter did not have a structured program and thus catered to women who preferred shelter space which had few expectations of its residents--i.e. the women who had been staying on the streets or at DESC before the shelter opened.

The things that the women liked about this shelter in comparison to the larger, primarily men's shelter they had been staying at were: its smaller size; the availability of locker space; the fact that smoking was not allowed inside; that a woman could keep her same bed night after night if she returned each night; that it was all women; that registration was for a longer period of time--from 5 pm to 7:30 pm rather than from 5 pm to 5:30 pm; that there were a few nice areas for sitting and reading; that the food was better--mostly because it was being served to a much smaller number of people; and that women could leave for a while in the evening and not lose their bed.

Criticisms about this program were mostly centered on the fact that it was temporary and thus would not always be available, that the beds were on the floor which was difficult for some of the women, and that it was closed during the day. Some of the women liked its downtown location, other women wanted a shelter that was outside of the downtown area.

DESC, the shelter which had been the primary unstructured program for single homeless women before the Women's Shelter opened, was fairly easy to criticize. Trying to house 250 people in a small space is a very difficult feat. Some of the things that bothered the women the most were: the noise, the smoke, the feeling of being unsafe as women--both when entering the shelter and while there--and the crowdedness. But some of the women, while being critical of certain aspects of this program, also truly appreciated it and were thankful for a place to stay where few demands were placed on them.

For those women I interviewed who had been staying at the shelters with more structured programs (e.g. LCC), the atmosphere of DESC or the Women's Shelter was hard to tolerate. On the other hand, some of the women who stayed at less structured shelters found the structured programs of other shelters to be too confining and too demanding. The women in my sample who had stayed in the structured programs were all women who went on to find housing during data collection. They were thankful for the help that they had gotten from counselors while staying at the shelters.

Angeline's, the drop-in center, was used by all but three of the women in my sample. The facilities for showers and doing laundry were well utilized and appreciated. Having a place to go during the day was essential for those women who stayed in the Women's Shelter--that closed during the day--and helpful for those who wanted to leave the crowded atmosphere of DESC during the day. It was also used by women who had their own rooms or apartments, as a place to socialize, do laundry, eat lunch and get services.

Different Reactions to Services

Some of the negative things said by women in the sample about services in general centered on a feeling that rules were too lax and people got away with things that left other people feeling unsafe. Carla in particular was always comparing the services in Seattle with what she had experienced in California. She thought that a stricter atmosphere would be beneficial. She was often frustrated by the philosophy of letting people be themselves without too many restrictions placed on them.

> I've been threatened in the bathroom, they steal stuff. But they [staff] bring it on. They don't do anything about it. . . . They [service users] are already so screwed up that they think they can push people around, call people filthy names. Angeline's doesn't do anything about it. It's the same thing at the Morrison [DESC], they don't do anything about it. And we're the victims. I told them that, because "you don't run it right". And this one woman who had her jaw broken said "That's right, Carla". . . . I thought they had stolen my ID. What made me angry was when I told P. [staff person], she said like "so what". . . . They don't seem to be able to make any changes. They are satisfied with the way it is.

She had her ideas of what would make things work better:

> They lack managerial qualities. That is a talent to be able to manage things well. In California they run those places like prisons, but it works. That's what you have to do when you are dealing with a segment of the population that does drugs, that carries knives, that threatens people. Someone threw something at me the other night because she said I was snoring, which I don't think I was. If you say something to them the words that come out of their mouths, I couldn't conjure up if I wanted to. . . . They need to bar people who don't cooperate. In California that is the way they do it and it works. You have to have set rules. People have to abide by them. It feels too strict but it works and you can go in there and feel safe because people won't swear at you and stuff.

Some of the criticism of services had to do with women feeling that they were not treated with respect nor as individuals. The following is an example of the sort of complaint a few of the women often made. It was generally hard to sort out in these instances whether the incident was due to personality clashes, overcrowding and understaffing, or a true lack of respect for the women.

> They [people in general] don't understand the pressure, they don't understand that no matter where you turn there is some slob coming up and putting you down, or if you are down they come and put the foot on your neck. They don't understand that because they've never been homeless so how would they know...It was only day before yesterday that I learned that they have cotton blankets...I have to have cotton because wool breaks me out. And I had understood from everybody that all cotton blankets had been reclaimed. I had had two letters from the doctors saying I had to have cotton blankets, wool blankets and I'd be in the hospital...He wrote a very severe letter. I only found out day before yesterday that they had cotton blankets. So I'm not mad at him [staff] but you can see why I don't believe him and I don't trust one word he says. It just burns me up...One time I said "You can please tell Mr. S. [administrator] that I'm sick and tired of carrying my cotton blankets around. I'm going to leave them here and you can wash them. I'm sick and tired of doing their work, they are getting the grant from the government." And I said "If you don't let me have the cotton blankets and if you bar me, that's fine. I will sleep on the grate, but I will be up very early and I'll be going over to the Department of Human Resources and I will tell them my story and while I'm up there I'll spill my guts about every other piece of shit."

One woman took advantage of an education/training program particularly for older homeless adults and enjoyed it quite a bit. Another woman went to the Senior Center, where she felt very comfortable, and took part in classes there. Another woman went to a day program for disabled adults at a city hospital. All of the above programs were free of charge to the women. Many of the women took advantage of free meals and events that happened regularly or for special holidays. Most of the women used the clothing banks and the food banks to help them save money. Many of the women went to doctors regularly and these relationships were central in their lives.

Some of the women were appreciative all the time of services they had used. Some of the women were appreciative of services some of the time and critical some of the time. And finally some of the women were critical all the time. All of them said that they would rather be living in their own home than in a shelter environment.

WHAT THE SERVICE PROVIDERS SAID

I interviewed 13 service providers: three were directors of programs specifically for homeless women; four were paraprofessional counselors in these programs; two were administrators--other than program directors--in agencies serving the homeless; two were mental health caseworkers who worked with homeless women; one was a nurse with Health Care for the Homeless; and one was an employee in the mayor's office with a responsibility to oversee the city's plan for assisting the homeless. All but one of the service providers that I interviewed felt very positively about their programs and what they had to offer homeless women. The dissenter felt that the program with which she worked needed a spiritual component. All the service providers spoke of the women with considerable caring, concern and respect. All of them thought that there was much more that needed to be done for homeless women.

Those staff that worked with the structured program felt that the counseling services they offered were important and helpful. The privacy their shelter offered the residents made it a more home-like atmosphere than the bigger shelters; this was something which they thought the women appreciated. One of their main problems was lack of space--they never had empty beds.

In the less structured programs and at the drop-in center the staff generally felt that they did a good job at respecting the women and letting them alone. As one staff person said:

> This may sound strange but one of the things that we do better than the other programs is that we just let them be. We don't put pressure on them. We don't limit how long they stay. We

don't require that they be making plans. We have been a kind of stable presence for some of the women on the streets.

One staff person with whom I spoke disagreed with this philosophy and felt that the women's spiritual needs were being neglected and that more structure was necessary to help women make changes in their lives.

I spoke with two mental health workers and one nurse who worked with homeless women. All three of them were overworked and felt the need for more services and resources for these women and homeless people in general. One of the mental health workers mentioned what a long process it was to gain trust and make progress with some of the women.

> What I am finding is that these women need to be able to tell their stories. They need to be believed. They really are products of our society. The systems are abusing them.

These service providers were all advocates for this population and so their visions for the future involved increased funding for housing and other services. They talked of the need for more shelter beds, and particularly shelter beds in small shelters serving only women. Affordable housing was mentioned by most of them, although they did not necessarily think that all these women would choose to live on their own, nor be happy alone. Many proposed housing situations that maintained a community atmosphere and had services available to the women. The limited treatment facilities for women with substance abuse issues, domestic violence issues, and mental health issues was also mentioned by several of the providers.

One service provider talked about her visions for the future that would respect diversity and give people an incentive to make changes. When I asked what her hopes were for this population, she said:

> I think definitely programs that are designed for specific populations, by disability, whatever. Because homeless people are diverse. We tend to have programs that are so general and it doesn't work. We need to have adequate funding especially for staff. If we start a program with inadequate staff it will never accomplish what it set out to accomplish. The welfare

system stinks. It doesn't give people incentives to change, it doesn't build their self esteem, but they need the money. You get penalized for working. That shouldn't be. If anything they should extend you [sic] and pat you on the back. People can't make it on minimum wage jobs. I think [programs need] to be culturally diverse. Programs tend to be white middle-class and the homeless population is not white middle-class. . . . Of course housing is a factor, but of course if we have housing we also have to have all these additional services. It has to be different types of housing once again and scattered in different areas. I don't think they should be ghettoized in certain areas. People are everywhere.

Group housing for older homeless women was mentioned several times:

Group housing with a counselor on staff would be better than just sticking them in an apartment and saying "So long you are on your own"...When you are homeless you have to fight every day and hide things. These women need a place of their own.

There must be some design that would meet their needs, that would give them companionship, and privacy and would give them a place to keep their things so that they were safe. That wouldn't cut them off from people.

Basically service providers felt they were doing a good job with the resources that they had. They had seen an increase in the number of older homeless women in the area in the past few years, but they also had seen that the city was trying to meet the increased demand, though many needs remained unmet.

Not surprisingly, service providers and homeless women, as consumers, have different perspectives on available services. The policy implications of these differing views are discussed in the final chapter.

CHAPTER 8

DISCUSSION AND POLICY IMPLICATIONS

INTRODUCTION

In this final chapter I examine the meaning of the four themes presented in the chapters on the women's past, present, and future lives. These themes: relationships, resiliency, normalcy and political awareness, emerged from the data and served as a framework for understanding the lives of the women in my sample. I comment upon how these findings are similar and different from previous research.

In the next section I discuss the similarities and differences between the views of service providers and the homeless women on current services for homeless women and visions for the future. I give suggestions on how the opinions of the homeless women in the sample might be used by service providers and program planners for the improvement of current services and the planning of future programs.

I will move from the specific issues brought up in my interviews with homeless women and service providers to discuss the broader policy implications of this research. I examine the areas of nutrition, health, income maintenance, employment, education and training, and housing for middle-aged and older homeless women.

Following this section on policy implications, I consider the questions that have emerged from this research. I suggest future research that could build upon this study by increasing our understanding of the service needs of middle-aged and older homeless women.

Before concluding, I touch upon how this research experience, and the relationships that I had with the eleven women, affected me personally as a feminist trying to do ethical research on an oppressed population.

THEMES FROM DATA

Relationships

Women's concern with relationships is a phenomenon that runs through our culture. Miller (1976) talks about women's ties to others as being a central part of their development.

> One central feature is that women stay with, build on, and develop in a context of attachment and affiliation with others. Indeed, women's sense of self becomes very organized around being able to make and then to maintain affiliations and relationships. Eventually, for many women the threat of disruption of an affiliation is perceived not as just a loss of a relationship but as something closer to total loss of self. (p. 83)

Perhaps one way the women in my sample guarded against this loss of self was by working hard to maintain ties to others despite the increased difficulty of this when living without a home.

In our society, women are the primary caregivers of children and dependent adults in both the domestic and public spheres (Abramovitz, 1988; Hanmer & Statham, 1989). So in some ways it is hardly surprising that the women in my sample also were focused on their family, friends and lovers. The surprise comes in part because the stereotype of an older homeless woman has been one of an isolated human being. And in fact when one does see a woman by herself, on the streets or in a shelter, with her possessions in bags or a shopping cart, a first thought is how lonely she looks.

Discussion and Policy Implications

It is possible that one of the limitations of my study which was mentioned earlier--that of my sample including only women who were already connected to services--comes into play in regard to relationships. The women in my sample may have more easily related to people and formed relationships than do homeless women that were not included in my sample. Service providers, who had worked with a much larger group of older, homeless women than I was able to know in my six month study period, frequently mentioned the ongoing importance of the personal losses they knew their clients to have experienced--loss of children, loss of lovers, loss of more comfortable life styles. They said that this was true for both the gregarious women and for the harder-to-reach women--those not in my sample--who required longer periods of time to form trusting relationships. For example, one woman, who I would see at Angeline's but who was not in my sample, kept her imaginary family with her everywhere she went and would consult with her imaginary husband and children on issues all day long.

Service providers mentioned on many occasions that giving a homeless woman an isolated room or small apartment was not necessarily the best housing option. They believed that some women were getting their community needs met, to some extent, through the shelter experience, and to take away the personal, daily interaction that happened in shelter living would leave a void in the women's lives. Only one woman in my sample articulated this feeling when she said that she needed to stay surrounded by people in order not to miss her family too much. Others spoke of wanting to live by themselves, partly so that they would have a place where they could have their children with them.

While some studies have mentioned the isolation of homeless women (Strasser, 1978; Anderson et al., 1988; Slavinski & Cousins, 1982) and the homeless mentally ill (Bassuk, 1984), others have noted that social ties do exist among the homeless.

Solarz and Bogat (1990) for example, found that the homeless individuals in their sample did have social support networks, though they were smaller and less satisfying than were those reported for domiciled populations. They concluded that building on an individual's natural support network could be one focus of intervention.

Although social support may not be the panacea of human problems that community psychologists have suggested, it is a particularly compelling focus for interventions involving the homeless and those at risk of homelessness. For example, fostering the mending of estranged social networks may facilitate the re-entry of homeless persons into housing by increasing resources for child care, transportation, information, possible financial support and emotional support.

Although I agree that interventions should include an awareness and sensitivity to homeless women's social support network, I do not think policies and programs should be focused on mending these ties at the expense of the structural changes that would keep a woman from being homeless in the first place.

Mitchell (1987) focused his study on the social ties of homeless women with an interest in whether people undergoing the crisis of homelessness were able to secure personal support from others to whom they were connected. In this study he examined the strength of relationship ties for ten women in a shelter for homeless families. He found the full range of ties from strong to weak for all the women in the sample. My own findings reflected this range of social ties.

After interviewing 35 homeless women in New York City, Coston (1989) found that almost one-half of her sample were never lonely.

> To these women, loneliness, appeared to be an emotion congruent with living on the streets that they did not appear to be aware of or at least, did not report. Furthermore, they reported being the loneliest when they were living in a manner condoned by society. (p.165)

Another quarter of her sample did report extreme loneliness with a desire to converse with the rest of society which they felt ignored them and victimized them.

Finally Berman-Rossi and Cohen (1989) reported on the success of a dinner group involving group process and shared decision making for women living in an SRO hotel. This activity brought otherwise isolated residents together for a regular community experience.

The significance of the theme of relationships is that no matter how difficult and perhaps marginal some of the relationships were or had been for the women in my sample, they remained an important part of each woman's identity. These women were not isolated individuals living in vacuums bereft of human contact. And even for those women whose relationships were troubling, the relationships were no less significant in the women's lives. Services for homeless women and near homeless women need to be sensitive to this aspect of their lives, both by building on the strength of women's relationship skills and, by assisting women to deal with the losses and pain they have experienced from relationships in their lives.

Resiliency

A stereotype which exists about people who receive public assistance is that they are lazy and dependent. Nine of the eleven women in my sample depended primarily on public assistance checks in the form of SSI or General Assistance, on their husband's pension check, or on Social Security Disability Insurance for their income. Physical, developmental, and psychiatric disabilities prevented these women from working at most jobs available in the labor market. The remaining two women had intermittent low-wage work throughout data collection. None of these women struck me as either dependent or lazy. Their daily lives required ingenuity and creativity in order for them to get their basic needs met.

One tenet of the profession of social work is to build on people's strengths. This certainly could be applied in the case of homeless women. Stark (1986) points this out when she advises developing facilities for the homeless, mentally ill that build on the skills they have developed from survival on the streets. Other authors have commented on how homeless women adopt creative behaviors that help them to survive on the streets (Strasser, 1978; Slavinski & Cousins, 1982), and how these behaviors need to be understood and respected. Similarly, the service providers interviewed for this study were, for the most part, cognizant of the resiliency of the homeless women they served, and attempted to offer services that did not detract from their independence and strengths.

Ultimately, while the resiliency of the women in my sample may be surprising to people who have had little contact with the homeless, it is not surprising for those who have worked with them or studied them. Stereotypes of dependent, lazy, people feeding off of society are disproved when one is exposed to the way these women deal with the hardships that are daily a part of their lives. The futility of the frequently touted conservative suggestion to "let them pull themselves up by their bootstraps" is clearly evident with this population of women who are indeed pulling hard, but not getting far. A deeper understanding of this by the public could lead to more humane public policies in the areas of housing, public assistance, and wages.

Normalcy

Perhaps one way that individuals who are not homeless are able to live with the fact that there are thousands and thousands of homeless people in this country, is to think of them as different. Blaming the victim is one attitude that is pervasive in our society. Our social welfare policies demonstrate this blaming the victim mentality: welfare benefits that are so punitively low that families cannot survive on them; unemployment benefits that are time-limited even in times of recession; guidelines for receiving disability benefits that so strict that many disabled people cannot qualify, are all examples of policies which punish people who have run into hard times. Perhaps as a society we are able to tolerate these policies as long as we think of those individuals that suffer their effects as different from ourselves.

The theme of normalcy that emerges from these data run counter to the notion that homeless women are somehow different from women who have homes. Merves (1986) discovered a similar theme in her data from interviews with 15 homeless women. She found

> .... the value systems of these women were not deviant from the dominant belief systems in the United States. These values included achievement, success, work, efficiency, progress, patriotism, private property, free enterprise, belief in a supreme being, and in particular for women family and children.

She goes on to say that none of us is that far from homelessness.

> Finally, the highly prized middle class status is precarious for increasing numbers of Americans. The long arduous journey to the middle class includes many roadblocks. Even once

attained middle class status is tenuous. In other words most people are closer to homelessness than they are to great wealth. The fall to homelessness for women is a much much shorter distance than the climb to the top.

It is a frightening thought to think that the line between being homeless and being housed is a fine one. It is more comfortable for those of us who are not homeless to believe that distinct differences exist between the two populations.

This theme of normality does not indicate that the women in the sample were all the same any more than women are all the same in society at large. Great diversity existed among the eleven women not unlike the diversity one finds in the dominant culture. For example, when war broke out in the Middle East during data collection, this diversity was well demonstrated. One woman was totally anti-war and very vocal about her distrust of our government's motives for going to war. Another woman was certain that the United States was taking the only morally justified action it could, by sending troops to the area, and had very negative things to say about anti-war activists. The other nine women fell somewhere in between these two extremes. Other people with whom I interacted during this Middle Eastern crisis demonstrated a similar range of reactions to the country's involvement. Another example of the diversity in this sample of older, homeless women which mirrors the diversity existing among housed, older women was that of the range of feelings about men. Some of the women felt distrustful and angry toward men and wanted to have little to do with them, while others claimed to prefer the company of men to that of women. The remaining women fell somewhere between.

The significance of this theme of normalcy is that as long as we hold certain populations to be somehow different and deviant, it will be easier to look for individual causes of homelessness rather than to the structural causes of poverty and lack of affordable housing.

Political Awareness

There does exist a small literature on the homeless organizing themselves in order to obtain basic rights such as shelter (Dreier & Atlas, 1989; Hombs & Snyder, 1986), but there has been no mention of political awareness in the literature specifically on homeless women. For this reason this final theme was perhaps the most surprising to me.

This theme challenges the notion of homeless women being passive victims who accept their fate without a fight. Though the level of awareness about the oppression they experienced in their lives varied among the women, none of them was blind to the inequities existing in our society nor to the fact that much about their lot in life was just not fair.

Several of the women viewed me as a part of the oppressive establishment and voiced that opinion occasionally. One woman asked me several times: "What are **you** going to do about these awful conditions anyway?". Another woman told me I was like "all the rest" and that I had absolutely no understanding about homelessness really, because I was not homeless myself. While these accusations were painful to hear, they indicated an anger at the system and at all those people connected to it.

This is an important finding in that it provides hope for collective action by homeless women in order to obtain better living conditions. Social workers interested in bringing about social change around issues such as housing should not underestimate the potential of older homeless women as change agents.

SERVICES FOR HOMELESS WOMEN: WHAT THE PROVIDERS AND CONSUMERS SAY

There were three primary areas of difference in my study between what the homeless women and what the service providers had to say about programs for the homeless. In most other instances it seemed as though there was a general consensus both about what worked well currently, and about how things could be better in the future, if only the resources existed. I will address the differences first and then discuss the commonalities.

The service providers whom I interviewed almost always talked about the homeless women whom they served with a great deal of respect and concern. (They also behaved this way when I observed them.) I felt that there was real caring for the women and a frustration about the lack of available resources to help them more. Every service provider whom I interviewed worked hard and was often stretched to

Discussion and Policy Implications

her limit. Most of the service providers I interviewed had been working with this population for years and felt they understood the general patterns, cycles and needs of the women generally, and that they knew the specifics of many of the women individually. In my hours of observation at Angeline's in particular I saw this caring demonstrated in the staff/consumer interactions time and time again.

Despite this apparent caring and respect, more than half of the homeless women spoke of being treated with disrespect by staff on occasion. For some of the women this was an ongoing dilemma that they spoke of at every interview. Sometimes it came as a blanket mistrust of a whole agency, sometimes it was focused at one particular staff person. This finding may come as no surprise to staff who are responsible for maintaining some sort of order in what are often chaotic situations, yet it warrants mentioning as it left some women feeling powerless and oppressed. It is possible that the staff who the homeless women found to be disrespectful were staff with whom I did not have contact. At DESC, in particular, the staff is large with some residents acting in almost staff-like positions as volunteers; one service provider mentioned to me that the quality of work from these volunteers varied enormously and at times they acted inappropriately with residents.

Another difference between what service providers said and what some homeless women said that surfaced in the interviews was how the "laissez-faire" atmosphere in the unstructured programs was viewed. The philosophy behind having minimal rules and few expectations of the consumers at Angeline's, the Women's Shelter and DESC, was to place the fewest restrictions possible on people who otherwise might not avail themselves of the services. Rules included: no physical or verbal abuse--including use of racist or sexist language; no weapons; no alcohol or drugs on the premises. Women could use the services while high if they were not disruptive, and were cooperating with staff.

All but one of the service providers interviewed, who worked in these three agencies, believed that this philosophy worked to keep the space safe and inviting for the greatest number of people. Yet some of the homeless women experienced this type of atmosphere as unsafe at times. They felt that some consumers should be "barred"--banned from the premises--for some of their behaviors including theft, bullying, and being high on drugs or alcohol. It is possible that some of the older women felt unsafe around the rowdiness of some of the younger women. Staff attributed this discomfort partially to cultural differences and racism--i.e.that white women were uncomfortable with the assertive behavior of some of the African American women. Some of the problems experienced by women at DESC were eliminated with the opening of the Women's Shelter which also provided a very unstructured program. The smaller size and the fact that it was for women only allowed for an atmosphere that felt safer and more comfortable for some of the women despite the same philosophy of few restrictions.

The final difference that emerged from the data on services had to do with thoughts about what homeless women wanted in terms of housing. None of the women articulated wanting to live in a community environment with services, if they could chose their preferred housing situation. This finding is similar to that found by Goering, Paduchak, and Durbin (1990) in a consumer preference survey they did of homeless women. When asked about housing preferences, only four of the 38 women interviewed by these authors said they would prefer living situations where meals and psychosocial services were provided. Similarly, the eleven women in this study all had dreams of living alone either in apartments or houses where they had full control over their lives. Service providers thought that for some women this would not work; they thought that the isolation and lack of contact with other residents and service providers would result in loneliness and an eventual return to the streets or shelters. It is possible that this difference is because when I asked the women what they would like as far as housing, they could not imagine a small, comfortable, community situation with services, as they have never known such a situation. Service providers knew that most of the women wanted to live on their own; they thought for some of the women this desire was unrealistic.

There were several areas where there was some consensus between what service providers and the homeless women mentioned in terms of services and housing. Both groups desired smaller shelters, and shelters just for women. One service provider even mentioned that perhaps there should be transitional housing particularly for older women. There was also a consensus on the need for storage space for homeless individuals. Easier access to treatment was mentioned by both of the women in my sample with current substance abuse issues; this was also mentioned by several service providers. The one woman in my sample who took advantage of mental health services provided by Health Care

Discussion and Policy Implications

for the Homeless appreciated these services; another woman felt like she needed counseling, but after she was housed did not know where she could find something she could afford. The mental health workers I spoke with felt overwhelmed by the number of individuals they had to see and the inability to do the thorough case management which they would have liked to do.

Public assistance checks that are too low to allow a person to pay unsubsidized monthly rent was mentioned by all the women surviving on these checks; service providers were well aware of this situation and thought that many of the women were making the intelligent choice to live in shelters and use their checks for day to day living. Subsidized housing was mentioned to be either unavailable or unlivable by both the homeless women and the service providers. Service providers were no less aware than the woman of how difficult it was to get employment at livable wages given the tight labor market and the low education and skill level of many of these women.

Generally I felt that service providers were true advocates for the women that they served. They felt as though their hands were tied in terms of the amount of help they could offer with so few resources. The differences expressed by the homeless women and service providers spelled out above could possibly disappear if more resources were available. The feeling of safety and respect is easier to foster in a smaller shelter environment with more staff that are well trained. It is possible that some of the women would in fact prefer a permanent living environment that was partially communal if they were also provided with a private room, storage space, and plenty of independence.

POLICY IMPLICATIONS

I came to this research with a fairly narrow view about the causes of homelessness. My bias was that homelessness was basically a problem of poverty and lack of affordable housing. Six months of immersion in the lives of homeless women, and contact with people who have been working with the issue for many years, has broadened my perspective considerably. I am much more willing to believe that homelessness is a complex problem involving more than lack of housing and income. But I also come away from this research with the belief that a federal commitment to provide housing and a liveable income for the entire population will be necessary in order to truly work at solving this problem. This will take considerable revenue.

Housing

Housing policies are the obvious place to begin when thinking about the policy implications of homelessness. Housing needs to become a national priority after a decade of neglect. As discussed in the literature review, homelessness is the inevitable result of the federal government's withdrawal of support for housing programs. In 1980, for every dollar spent on housing the federal government spent seven dollars on defense, by 1988 this ratio had increased to forty dollars on defense for every dollar on housing. Housing programs were slashed from over 33 billion dollars to less than eight billion dollars during the Reagan administration (Dreier & Atlas, 1989).

Making a commitment to house the poor will in fact take revenue. This revenue could come from withdrawing some of the housing subsidies enjoyed by the wealthy in this country:

> The one housing subsidy that did not fall to President Reagan's budget axe is the one that goes to the very rich. The federal tax code allows homeowners to deduct all property tax and mortgage interest from their income taxes. This cost the federal government $35.1 billion in forgone revenues in 1987 alone, according to the Congressional Budget Office. This amount is more than four times the HUD budget for low-income housing. Two-thirds of the forgone tax revenue goes to the 10.7 percent of taxpayers who earn over $50,000 annually. One quarter of this subsidy goes to the two percent of taxpayers with annual incomes over $100,000. One half of all homeowners do not claim deductions at all. In other words, our nation's housing subsidies disproportionately benefit homeowners with high incomes or with more than one home. (Dreier & Atlas, 1989, pp.29-30)

To channel some portion of the $35.1 billion of forgone revenues mentioned above into housing subsidies for the poor would go a long way to easing the problem of homelessness in this country.

Not only is there a lack of housing for the poor, but the low-income housing that does exist is often substandard. Many of the women in my study preferred shelter living to spending most of their income on rooms or apartments which were not much better than the shelter environments. Financial incentives to private developers could be provided by the federal government to build and adequately maintain quality subsidized and low-income housing. This was done in the 1960's and 1970's and resulted in the creation of over two million low-income apartments. Unfortunately many of these apartment buildings were poorly run and maintained. To make matters worse, developers were given the option of converting these subsidized apartment buildings to market-rate apartments after twenty years--this is happening currently and has contributed to the loss of low-income housing and displacement of families (Dreier & Atlas, 1989). New housing policies should take these mistakes from the 60's into account so that subsidized housing is not only well maintained but also permanent.

Current federal reactions to the homeless have centered on shelters--band-aid solutions rather than preventative measures. With the ever increasing rate of homelessness, more shelters are in fact needed. Transitional housing--another focus of some government funding--that includes services for residents may be appropriate for some portion of the homeless population. But policy makers need to know that shelters often become more than just emergency housing for some residents--several of the women in my sample had "lived" in shelters for years. Clearly, until there is adequate housing, shelters will remain necessary in order to give homeless people options other than living on the streets. If we are going to continue to use shelters as a stopgap measure, they can at least be more humane. Smaller facilities that cater to certain segments of the homeless population--e.g. women, men, families, youth--with adequate storage and areas for personal hygiene are preferable over large warehouses that try to shelter hundreds of adults each night.

Income Maintenance

The nine women in my sample who had fixed incomes survived on monthly checks that ranged from about $350 (General Assistance, GA) to about $600 (Social Security Disability Insurance, SSDI), with most of them receiving about $420 (Supplemental Security Income, SSI). GA amounts vary from state to state but tend to be lower than federal checks such as SSI, and SSDI varies depending upon a person's work history. Two women in my sample who were living on fixed incomes were able to secure housing during the data collection period. One woman was able to afford a small one bedroom apartment by combining her SSI check with her boyfriend's SSD check. The other woman paid more than half of her $500 monthly income in order to rent a small room. The other seven women were unable to find affordable housing given their income limitations.

Living on such small incomes required a great deal of ingenuity and sacrifice. Generally the end of the month was a time of little money when they would rely, to an even greater extent, on free meals and food banks. All the women, both those who rented and those who remained in shelters throughout data collection, rationed out their checks over the month the best that they could. Only one of the women seemed to spend her money "foolishly" by taking a week's vacation at the beginning of the month and then being penniless for the remainder. Others bought themselves warm boots--the one clothing item which was hard to get at clothing banks--bought their children clothes and small gifts, bought cigarettes, treated themselves to cups of coffee or cheap breakfast at restaurants. The five dollar payments that I gave them at our interviews were always appreciated and needed.

It is unreasonable to expect people to be able to meet their basic needs on such punitively small public assistance checks. Even those individuals that are fortunate enough to secure subsidized housing have a difficult time making ends meet. The blaming the victim attitude mentioned earlier has resulted in policies that penalize people who are dependent on society due to disability and old age. A more humane policy would raise the SSI benefit level to one on which a person could comfortably live, and ease guidelines for receiving SSI. Currently people who are unable to support themselves due to disability but who are denied SSI either have no income or receive temporary assistance through the state-run, poorly funded GA programs.

Employment/Education and Training

Two women in my sample were employed intermittently throughout the data collection period. At the end of data collection they were both working at low-skill jobs where they earned less than $6 per hour, a cut in pay for both of them. One was working full-time and the other about 30 hours a week. Both of them were in rental situations at the end of data collection and both were behind on their rent and depending on outside sources for grocery money and food.

One woman felt that she was working well below her skill level and that she had experienced age discrimination in her search for employment. The other woman was hopeful that she would be able to land a job that paid a higher wage though her skills were limited. Higher wages and job security would improve the situation for both of these women. Enforced affirmative action policies would be helpful in the area of age or sex discrimination, and employment training programs might be helpful for improving the skill level for some middle-aged impoverished women. The danger of emphasizing training programs is that jobs paying liveable wages are not always available in which to place the newly trained participants.

One woman in the sample was taking advantage of education and training programs targeted at homeless individuals. She enjoyed the process of studying for her GED and it seemed to enrich her life. She had hopes of moving into a training program that would increase her job skills so that she could eventually work at a job that interested her and paid her an adequate wage. Her employment experience included only low-wage, low-skill work which she could no longer do due to physical disabilities. Several of the women who received public assistance spoke to me about wanting to work, and wanting to get training to do more interesting work than what they had done in the past. Education and training programs that meet these women where they are and build on their strengths and experiences would allow society to take advantage of the talents of an often invisible population.

Health

For the majority of the women in the sample doctor visits were an important part of their daily life. Some of these women had chronic conditions that needed regular attention. Most of the women received Medicaid and thus were able to obtain the prescribed drugs and to tend to their medical needs. Several of the women did not have medical insurance and this caused them to neglect some of their health needs and to worry about unpaid medical bills. A couple of the women and several service providers mentioned that even with Medicaid, choice about medical care was much more limited for impoverished individuals than for people with greater financial resources.

Certainly a national health insurance program that would cover all low-income individuals would be helpful for many homeless women who are struggling to survive on low-wage work or on pensions that put them above the eligibility level for Medicaid. Two women in the sample spoke of wanting to go into treatment for substance abuse during the data collection period. Neither of these women had health insurance and the cost of such programs put treatment out of the range of possibility for both of them. Easier access to treatment is of great importance to some members of the homeless population--including older homeless women.

Nutrition

Limited income results in less choice about diet. Women in my sample who lived in shelters often spoke of the starchiness of the institutional food on which they depended. Many of them would talk about their weight, and a couple often were trying to diet. One dietary concern of older women is getting an adequate amount of calcium--this is difficult to do when depending on free meals at shelters. Most of the women did not have the resources to get daily fresh fruits and vegetables, although some of them would spend portions of their small checks on healthy food to supplement what they were served at the shelters.

Many of the women, both those in shelters and those who had housing, took advantage of the food banks to help them stretch their monthly income. These food banks were not able to carry very much fresh food. Both homeless and marginally housed women took advantage of the snacks and cold lunches served at Angeline's. Churches would provide large free dinners on holidays and other occasions which the women took advantage of and seemed to enjoy. Smaller shelters seemed to be able to provide tastier and fresher meals than was possible when trying to feed hundreds of people at once. One homeless woman said to me that she thought that shelters should ask supermarkets to donate the produce that they tossed out daily.

Most nutrition programs in this country are focused on pregnant women, babies and young children. Meals on Wheels is one program that serves the older population. Service providers did mention using this program for women living alone in SRO's. They were worried that the women were not adequately feeding themselves. Most of the women received some amount of food stamps which supplemented their small incomes.

Ultimately, adequate income and housing seem to be the best policies to meet the nutrition needs of this population. Income gives the women more choice about what they eat and allows them to buy fresh food for themselves, and housing allows them a place to store it and cook it. Many of the women spoke of wanting to be able to cook for themselves, something that is only possible when they have housing. It is much easier to efficiently use food stamps, or for that matter to buy groceries with money, when one has a kitchen, a refrigerator, and a place to store food.

FUTURE RESEARCH

The theme of political awareness was a relatively surprising one and warrants further investigation. Comments by several women about the collective action taken by homeless individuals in Seattle during data collection made me wonder about what role women play in such events. One woman mentioned to me that "these things are always run by men" but I wonder to what extent women have been involved. A question about the eviction process comes to mind after hearing several of the women talk about how they dealt with being evicted from their apartments by landlords whom they felt had not held up their end of the tenant/landlord bargain. It would be interesting to know how successful women have been in their legal fights and also how many women feel they were illegally evicted and thus now homeless. And finally, I heard a few stories about managers in SRO hotels who were sexually inappropriate with female renters. It would be useful to know how frequent a problem this is, and how women generally deal with it.

Another area that deserves further exploration is that of transitional housing and community housing for older, homeless women. Many service providers suggested this as one important option for older, single homeless women, although the women rarely suggested it themselves. It would be interesting to interview women who currently live in transitional housing to understand the things that they like and don't like, and to see what works well and what does not. One woman in my sample moved from a shelter into a housing situation that could be called transitional in that the rent was cheap and she could stay there three years. No services were attached to this situation. It would be interesting to know what has happened to the women who have had rooms in this facility and whether they have been able to go on to more permanent living situations. Service providers also often mentioned that they knew of times when older, single women were placed into permanent housing situations when these placements didn't work out for one reason or another. Service providers thought that there was something about the shelter or street life style that these women missed. It would be interesting to explore this issue further.

My sample of older homeless women was recruited from shelters in a downtown area of a large city. It would be interesting to do a similar study in a rural area or a suburban area to see what differences and similarities might exist. One segment of the homeless population which I did not access were women who are not in contact with services. I am unsure whether these are women who would be willing to talk with a researcher or not, but it would be useful to hear their stories. It would also be interesting to know more about the people who are living in cars, vans, and camper trailers. I am not sure if this is something that single homeless women do or not. The city official I interviewed mentioned that the city was interested in knowing more about this population.

Within my sample there were many commonalities and differences between the women. Some of the women were substance abusers, some had experience with domestic violence, some had experienced psychiatric hospitalizations, and some had physical disabilities. It would be interesting to have a larger sample of older, homeless women

Discussion and Policy Implications

and to make some comparisons between these various subpopulations. Service needs and housing options may differ considerably for the different groups.

Finally I am personally interested in the fate of the eleven women with whom I spent six months of my life. I would be very interested to know in six months or a year's time about how they have managed in the interim period, what was going on for them then, and what their plans and hopes were for the future. I heard from and responded to four of the women in the year after data collection; I am no longer in contact with any of them. This saddens me and reminds me of the distance that was never quite bridged between researcher and informant, something I expand on below.

MY PERSONAL REACTIONS TO THIS RESEARCH EXPERIENCE

Shortly after I completed my data collection I was introduced to a book on feminist research that included a chapter on issues of epistemology and methodology in feminist sociological research (Cook & Fonow, 1990). The authors listed five epistemological principles they consider to guide feminist methodology which I found helpful in understanding my own experience as a feminist trying to do research with an oppressed group of women. They include:

1. the necessity of continuously and reflexively attending to the significance of gender and gender asymmetry as a basic feature of all social life, including the conduct of research;
2. the centrality of consciousness-raising as a specific methodological tool and as a general orientation or "way of seeing";
3. the need to challenge the norm of objectivity that assumes that the subject and object of research can be separated from one another and that personal and /or grounded experiences are unscientific;
4. concern for the ethical implications of feminist research and recognition of the exploitation of women as objects of knowledge; and
5. emphasis on the empowerment of women and transformation of patriarchal social institutions through research. (pp. 72-73)

The fourth and fifth principles were the two that spoke to me most strongly as I dealt with some of my feelings of discomfort in doing this research project, but I will begin by discussing the first three principles. There were many times throughout data collection and analysis when I wondered whether I was learning anything that was of any worth to anyone. I attribute this questioning partly to the devaluation of women and their experiences in this society--principle number one--and the lack of emphasis in academia on grounded experience as a source of knowledge--principle three. It was primarily through talking with interested friends and colleagues that I maintained a sense of the value of the research that I was doing--people that considered the telling of these women's stories to be important and necessary.

Because of the political awareness of many of the women in my sample, consciousness-raising--principle number two--generally went in both directions. I found that I did some consciousness-raising with the women who had ongoing issues with abusive relationships, and some supportive listening for those with current issues with substance abuse, but over all I was in the position of learning about discrimination and oppression from women who were very conscious of experiencing it themselves.

Principle number four was perhaps the most troubling for me. I was ever aware that I was in a more powerful position than the women in that I had money, I had housing, I could leave at the end of the interview to go to a more comfortable environment. Some of the women let me know on occasion that they saw me as an oppressor and as a part of the system that was oppressing them. They would do this either indirectly, by asking me what I was going to do about the situation, or directly, by telling me that there was no way that I could understand what it meant to be homeless because I wasn't homeless.

With five of the women, friendships developed that had a nice quality of give and take in that, as I learned of their lives, they appeared happy to have a new friend who cared about what they had to say. Three woman were fairly volatile or unpredictable and I never knew quite what to expect from them; I learned to use certain behaviors in order not to irritate them too much. One woman was developmentally disabled and there always existed an imbalance in our relationship because of that, but I think she enjoyed our meetings, and certainly looked forward to the five dollar payments. And one woman I only met with one time so there was not opportunity to develop an ongoing relationship.

Since the time of the termination interviews I have missed all of the women and wondered about them often. I feel some discomfort about having dropped into their lives for six months and then totally removed myself. I am grappling with the feelings that come with the recognition that I have in fact exploited these women as objects of knowledge.

The final principle listed by these authors has to do with action research--research that leads to participation, empowerment and social change. I believe that my applause and affirmation of the women when they told me of the actions they had taken in their lives to deal with oppressive situations were empowering. I also believe my acknowledgement and confirmation of their feelings of discrimination was also empowering on some level. Still, I am unsure how this research will bring about social change. Because my personal goal for this research and any research is to work toward the transformation of oppressive institutions, I feel unsettled in not knowing if my work will in anyway improve the lives of the women I was privileged to know through this research.

CONCLUSION

The purpose of this research was to understand more about the lives and service needs of older, single homeless women. Impoverished, middle-aged women have received little public or academic attention in the past. This research indicated that homeless women in this age group do have some particular service needs.

While eight of the women in my sample were able to receive small public assistance checks due to disabilities, most of them would have liked to have had part time employment to supplement these checks, if they could have done so without losing their public assistance eligibility. Education and training programs targeted at middle-aged women and a more flexible labor market that could absorb individuals with disabilities would be helpful to this population. Our society has tended to undervalue older, unemployed women; they have many talents and extensive experience to offer.

Middle-aged women without children or disabilities do not qualify for subsidized housing. This makes it even more difficult for these women to attain affordable housing. Universal housing, subsidies for all individuals or families who pay more than one third of their income for rent, would remedy this problem.

Similarly, middle-aged women without children or severe disabilities do not qualify for public assistance. This leaves a group of women without income if they are unable to secure employment. Some women are unable to maintain employment due to disabilities, and yet they are also unable to receive public benefits because their disabilities are not "severe enough". Again, a universal income for all individuals would prevent certain needy segments of our nation's population from falling through the cracks of the social welfare safety net.

And finally, as long as shelters are necessary, small shelters with programs designed particularly for older, single women would allow this population the privacy, safety, and care they deserve. In Seattle, shelters exist for homeless families, for older men, for women and families, for single women of all ages, for men of all ages, for single adults. No shelter serves only older, single women. My sense is that the women in my sample would have appreciated such a facility.

The first three themes which emerged from interviews with the eleven middle-aged, homeless women in this study give evidence that these women are not unlike other middle-aged women in our society. Relationships and affiliation are important in their lives. They deal with hardships and challenges resiliently and with good humor. Their past, their day to day lives, and their hopes for the future include very normal behaviors, feelings, and plans that make this group indistinguishable from other low-income women at midlife. The final theme, political awareness, gives hope for collective action by older, homeless--and near homeless--women to demand fairer and more humane social policies.

REFERENCES

Abramovitz, M. (1988). *Regulating the lives of women: Social welfare policy from colonial times to the present.* Boston: South End Press.

Anderson, S.C., Boe, T. & Smith, S. (1988). Homeless women. *Affilia, 3*(2), 62-70.

Bachrach, L.L. (1985). Chronic mentally ill women: Emergence and legitimation of program issues. *Hospital and Community Psychiatry, 36*(10), 1063-1069.

Bachrach, L.L. (1987). Homeless women: A context for health planning. *The Milbank Quarterly, 65*(3), 371-396.

Barak, G. (1991). *Gimme shelter: A social history of homelessness in contemporary America.* New York: Praeger.

Bassuk, E.L., Rubin, L., & Lauriat, A, (1984). Is homelessness a mental health problem? *American Journal of Psychiatry, 141*(12), 1546-50.

Baum, A.S. & Burnes, D. W. (1993). *A nation in denial: The truth about homelessness.* Boulder CO: Westview Press.

Baxter, E. & Hopper, K. (1981). *Private lives\public spaces.* New York: Community Service Society.

Benda, B.B. & Dattalo, P. (1990). Homeless women and men: Their problems and use of services. *Affilia, 5*(3), 50-82.

Bergmann, B. (1986). *The economic emergence of women.* New York: Basic Books, Inc., Publishers.

Berlin, S.B. & Jones, L.E. (1983). Life after welfare: AFDC termination among long-term recipients. *Social Service Review, 57*(3), 279-303.

Berman-Rossi, T. & Cohen, M.B. (1988). Group development and shared decision making working with homeless mentally ill women. *Social Work with Groups, 11*(4), 63-78.

Blau, J. (1992). *The visible poor: Homelessness in the United States.* New York: Oxford University Press.

Block, M.R., Davidson, J.L. & Grahms, J.D. (1981). *Women over forty.* New York: Springer Publishing Co.

Breton, M. (1988). The need for mutual-aid groups in a drop-in for homeless women: The sistering case. *Social Work with Groups, 11*(4), 47-61.

Brody, E.M. (1981). Women in the middle and family help to older people. *The Gerontologist, 21*(5), 471-480.

Brown, K.S. & Ziefert, M. (1990). A feminist approach to working with homeless women. *Affilia, 5*(1), 6-20.

Butler, S.S. & Weatherley, R.A. (1992). Poor women at midlife and the categories of neglect. *Social Work, 37*, 510-516.

Cahn, A.F. (Ed.). (1978). *Women in midlife--Security and fulfillment (part 1)* (Comm. Pub 95-170). Washington DC: US Government Printing Office.

Center on Budget and Policy Studies. (1985). *Smaller pieces of the pie.* Washington DC: Center on Budget and Policy Studies.

Chenitz, W.C. & Swanson, J.M. (Eds.). (1986). *From practice to grounded theory.* Menlo Park, CA: Addison-Wesley Publishing Co.

Cook, J.A. & Fonow, M.M. (1990). Knowledge and women's interests: Issues of epistemology and methodology in feminist sociological research. In J.M. Nielsen (Ed.), *Feminist research methods: Exemplary readings in the social sciences* (pp. 69-93). Boulder, CO: Westview Press.

Corrigan, E.M. & Anderson, S.C. (1984). Homeless alcoholic women on skid row. *American Journal of Drug and Alcohol Abuse, 10*(4), 535-549.

Coston, C.T.M. (1989). The original designer label: Prototypes of New York City's shopping bag ladies. *Deviant Behavior, 10,* 157-172.

Denzin, N.K. (1978). *The research act: A theoretical introduction to sociological methods.* New York: McGraw-Hill Book Co.

Dreier, P. & Atlas, J. (1989). Grassroots strategies for the housing crisis: A national agenda. *Social Policy, 19*(3), 25-38.

Fabricant, M.B. (1990). Counting the homeless. *A Journal of Reviews and Commentary in Mental Health, 5*(1), 16-20.

Garrett, G.R. & Bahr, H.M. (1976). The family backgrounds of skid row women. *Signs: Journal of Women in Culture and Society, 2*(2), 369-381.

Goering, P., Paduchak, D. & Durbin, J. (1990). Housing homeless women: A consumer preference study. *Hospital and Community Psychiatry, 41*(6), 790-794.

Gilchrist, L. (1990). *Emergency shelter users in Washington state.* Published report available from Corrine Foster, Department of Community Development, Ninth and Columbia Building, MS/Gh-51, Olympia, WA 98504-4151

Glaser, B.G. (1978). *Theoretical sensitivity.* Mill Valley, CA: The Sociology Press.

Glaser, B.G. & Strauss, A.L. (1967). *The discovery of grounded theory.* New York: Aldine Publications, Co.

Golden, S. (1992). *The women outside.* Berkeley: University of California Press.

Golden, S. (1990). Lady versus low creature: Old roots of current attitudes toward homeless women. F*rontiers, 11*(2/3),1-7.

Gottlieb, N. (1989). Families, work and the lives of older women. In J.D. Garner and S.O. Mercer (Eds.), *Women as they age: Challenge, opportunity and triumph* (pp.217-244). New York: The Haworth Press.

Hagen, J.L. & Ivanoff, A.M. (1988). Homeless women: A high-risk population. *Affilia, 3*(1), 19-33.

Hand, J.E. (1983). Shopping bag women of Manhattan. (Doctoral dissertation, New School for Social Research, 1982). *Dissertation Abstracts International, 43*, 4309A.

Hanmer, J. & Statham, D. (1989). *Women and social work: Towards a woman-centered practice.* Chicago: Lyceum Books, Inc.

Hartman, C. (1983). Introduction: A radical perspective on housing reform. In C. Hartman (Ed.), *America's housing crisis: What is to be done?.* Boston: Routledge & Kegan Paul.

Hombs, M.E. & Snyder, M. (1986). *Homelessness in America: A forced march to nowhere.* Washington DC: Community for Creative Nonviolence.

Hooyman, N. (1989, March). *Gender, caregiving and equity: A feminist perspective.* Invitational paper presented at the annual program meeting of the Council of Social Work Education, Chicago, Illinois.

Hopper, K., Baxter, E. Cox, S. & Klein, L. (1982). *One year later, the homeless poor in New York City, 1982.* New York: Community Service Society.

Hopper, K. & Hamberg, J. (1984). *The making of America's homeless: From Skid Row to new poor.* New York: Community Service Society.

Human Services Strategic Planning Office (1989). *Status of homelessness in the city of Seattle.* Seattle, Washington.

Institute of Medicine. (1988). *Homelessness, health and human needs.* Washington D.C.: National Academy Press.

Johnson, A.K. & Kreuger, L.W. (1989). Toward a better understanding of homeless women. *Social Work, 34*(6), 537-540.

Karger, H.J. & Stoesz, D. (1990). *American social welfare policy: A structural approach.* New York: Longman.

Katz, M.B. (1989). *The undeserving poor: From the war on poverty to the war on welfare.* New York: Pantheon Books.

Kirk, J. & Miller, M.L. (1986). *Reliability and validity in qualitative research.* Beverly Hills, CA: Sage Publications.

Koegel, P. (1986, October). *Ethnographic perspectives on homeless and homeless mentally ill women.* Proceedings of a two-day workshop sponsored by the Division of Education and Service Systems Liaison National Institute of Mental Health. Washington, D.C.

Kozol, J. (Speaker). (1989). *At the mercy of America: The homeless and their children.* NASW Annual Convention, San Francisco.

Kutza, E.A. & Keigher, S.M. (1991). The elderly "new homeless": An emerging population at risk. *Social Work, 36*(4), 288-293.

Kutza, E.A. (1978). Passed over by progress: Women at the bottom. In A.F. Cahn, *Women in midlife--security and fulfillment* (pp.222-236) (Comm. Pub. 95-170). Washington, DC: US Government Printing Office.

Levine, T.S. & Rog, D. J. (1990). Mental health services for homeless mentally ill persons. *American Psychologist, 45*(8), 963-968.

Liebow, E. (1993). *Tell them who I am: The lives of homeless women.* New York: The Free Press.

Lopata, H.Z. & Brehm, H.P. (1986). *Widows and dependent wives: From social problem to federal program.* New York: Praeger.

McIntyre, R.S. (1988). The Populist Tax Act of 1986. *The Nation, 246*(13), 445.

Marcuse, P. (1983, April). Homelessness is a product. *Christianity and Crisis*, pp.129-134.

Martin, M. (1982). Strategies of adaptation: Coping patterns of the urban transient female. (Doctoral dissertation, Columbia University, 1982). *Dissertation Abstracts International, 43,* 4305A.

Merves, E. (1986). Conversations with homeless women: A sociological examination: Summary report. (Doctoral dissertation, Ohio State University, 1986). *Dissertation Abstracts International, 47,* 4705A.

Milburn, N. & D'Ercole, A. (1991). Homeless women: Moving toward a comprehensive model. *American Psychologist, 46*(11), 1161-1169.

Miles, M.B. & Huberman, A.M. (1984). *Qualitative data analysis.* Beverly Hills, CA: Sage Publications.

Miller, J.B. (1976). *Toward a new psychology of women.* Boston, Beacon Press.

References

Mitchell, J.C. (1987). The components of strong ties among homeless women. *Social Networks, 9,* 37-47.

Multnomah County, Oregon. (1984). *The homeless poor.* Portland, Oregon: Department of Human Services.

Multnomah County, Oregon. (1985). *Homeless women.* Portland, Oregon: Department of Human Services.

Nuccio, K.E. (1989). The double standard of aging and older women's employment. In J.D. Garner and S.O. Mercer (Eds.), *Women as they age: Challenge, opportunities, and triumph* (pp.317-338). New York: The Haworth Press.

Piven, F.F. & Cloward, R.A. (1971). *Regulating the poor: The functions of public welfare.* New York: Vintage Books.

Pearce, D. M. (1988). *The invisible homeless: Women and children* (prepared for Locked Out: Women and Housing). Washington DC: Institute for Women's Policy Research.

Ridgeway, J. (1984, February, 14). The administration's attack on the homeless: Building a fire under Reagan. *Village Voice.*

Reagan on homelessness: Some choose life out there. (1988, December). *New York Times.* pp. 1, 12.

Roberts, R.E. & Keefe, T. (1986). Homelessness: Residual, institutional and communal solutions. *Journal of Sociology and Social Welfare, 13* (2), 400-417.

Rousseau, A.M. (1981). *Shopping bag ladies: Homeless women speak about their lives.* New York: Pilgrim Press.

Schatzman, L. & Strauss, A.L. (1973). *Field research: Strategies for a natural sociology.* Englewood Cliffs, NJ: Prentice-Hall, Inc.

Select Committee on Aging. (1980). *The status of mid-life women and options for their future.* (Comm. Pub. 96-215). Washington DC: U.S. government Printing Office.

Scott, H. (1984). *Working your way to the bottom: The feminization of poverty.* Boston: Pandora Press.

Shulman, A.K. (1981). Preface. In A.M. Rousseau, *Shopping bag ladies* (pp.10-12). New York: Pilgrim Press.

Slavinsky, A.T. & Cousins, A. (1982). Homeless women. *Nursing Outlook, 30*(6), 358-362.

Solarz, A. & Bogat G.A. (1990). When social supports fail: The homeless. *Journal of Community Psychology, 18,* 79-96.

Sommers, T. & Shields, L. (1978). Problems of the displaced homemaker. In A.F. Cahn (Ed.) *Women in midlife--security and fulfillment* (pp.86-106) (Comm. Pub. 95-170). Washington DC: US Government Printing Office.

Stark, L.R. (1986). Strangers in a strange land. *International Journal of Mental Health, 14*(4), 95-111.

Stoner, M.R. (1983). The plight of homeless women. *Social Service Review, 57,* 565-581.

Strasser, J.A. (1978). Urban transient women. *American Journal of Nursing, 78,* 2076-2079.

Strauss, A. L. (1987). *Qualitative analysis for social scientists.* New York: Cambridge University Press.

Sullivan, M.A. (1991). The homeless older woman in context: Alienation, cutoff and reconnection. *Journal of Women & Aging, 3*(2), 3-24.

Swanson-Kauffman, K.M. (1986). A combined qualitative methodology for nursing. *Advances in Nursing Sciences, 8*(3), 58-69.

Swanson-Kauffman, K.M. & Schonwald, E. (1988). Phenomenology. In B.Sarter (Ed.), *Paths to knowledge: Innovative research methods for nursing* (pp.97-105) . New York: National League for Nursing.

The Women and Poverty Project. (1989). *Women and housing fact sheet*. Washington DC: Institute for Women's Policy Research.

US Bureau of the Census. (1991). *Poverty in the United States: 1990* (Current Population Reports, Series P-60, No 175). Washington DC:U.S. Government Printing Office.

Wright, J.D. (1988). The worthy and unworthy homeless. *Society, 25*(5), 64-69.

INDEX

A
abortion, 61
Abramovitz, M., 118
abuse, 69 (also see battered women, sexual abuse)
advocates, 9, 127
AFDC, 4, 18 (see also welfare benefits)
affordable housing, (see low-income housing)
African Americans, 14, 19, 41-42, 49, 126
Albany, NY, 13-14
alcohol treatment (see substance abuse treatment)
alcoholism (see substance abuse)
alienation (see isolation)
American Psychological Association (APA), xiv, 9
Anderson, S., 8, 13-14, 119
Angeline's, 26-28, 29, 31, 38, 72, 109-111, 125, 133
Angie, 41-42, 48-49, 52, 70-71, 77-78, 83, 87-88, 97-98
aspirations (see future plans)
Atlas, J., xxi, 5-7, 123, 128-129
attrition, 31

B
Bachrach, L., xxi, 1, 7
bag lady, xxi, 16-17, 118
Bahr, H., 8
Barak, G., xv
Bassuk, E., 7, 119
battered women, 8, 11, 26, 41-42, 48-50, 57-58, 61,67,70-71, 77, 81, 87-88, 93, 96, 114, 136
Baum, A., xv
Baxter, E., xxi, 1, 8-9
Beatrice, 30, 31, 42, 50, 55-56, 71, 72-73, 78, 94, 101
Benda, B., xiv
Bergmann, B., 18
Berlin, S., 18
Berman-Rossi, T., 15-16, 120
bills, 55-56, 77-78, 97, 100
blacks (see African Americans)
Blau, J., xvi-xvii
Block, M., 18
block grants, 10-11
Boe, T., 13-14, 119
Bogat, G., 119-120
Boston, 6
boyfriends (see lovers)
Brehm, H., 18
Breton, M., 15
Brinkley, D., 12
Brody, E., 18
Brown, K., xii
bum, xxi
Burnes, D., xv
Butler, S., xiv, 18
Bykofsky, S., 12

C

Cahn, A., 18
California, 57, 61-62, 111
capitalism, xv, 103
caregiving, 18, 118
Carla, 42, 53, 61-63, 67-68, 73-74, 79, 85, 88-89, 97, 98-99, 102-105, 111
cars, 74-75
case worker, 59, 89
Catholic Community Services, 37
causes of homelessness, 1-8
Center on Budget and Policy Studies, 2
Chenitz, W., 34, 35
child support, 61-62
childhoods, 51-54,
children, 32, 41-44, 51, 58, 66-69, 87-94, 101, 119 (see also sons, daughters)
Christmas (see holidays)
church, 81, 133
class structure (See capitalism, lower class, middle class, upper class)
clothes, 73, 82, 113
Cloward, R., 4
coalitions, xvii
Cohen, M., 15-16, 120
Columbus, OH, 17
community, 115, 119, 126
compensation, 30
confidentiality, 32, 39
Congress, 7, 105
consent form, 39
constant comparative analysis, 24, 33-34

Cook, J., 135
Corrigan, E., 8
counselors, (see mental health treatment)
Coston, M., 120
counting the homeless, xxi-xxii
Cousins, A., 8, 13, 119, 121
Cox, S., 9
cross-sectional research, xxiii-xxiv, 24
cutbacks in social welfare, xxiii, 4

D

D'Ercole, A., xiv
data analysis, 33-34, 37
data collection, 26-32, 36-38
dating, 88, 89, 92, 98
Dattalo, P., xiv
daughters, 50, 52, 66-69, 82, 88-89, 102
Davidson, J., 18
day-to-day lives, 65-85
deindustrialization, xvi, xxiii, 2-3, 18
deinstitutionalization, 7-8
delimiting themes, 24, 33-34, 37
Denzin, N., 23, 31
DESC, 26-28, 29, 31, 38, 60, 73-74, 75, 94, 109-111, 125, 126
descriptive surveys, 13-15
Dierdra, 42, 59-60, 71, 73, 79-80, 89-90, 100-101
disability/disabled, 4, 18, 42-44, 45, 48, 53, 54-55, 59-60, 61-63, 74-75, 98, 101, 105, 107, 112, 121, 132, 136, 137-138

Index

discrimination, 57, 59, 60, 61-63, 83, 105, 106, 107, 131, 136
diversity, xv, xxiii, 24-25, 26, 115, 123, 125-126, 134
divorce, xxiii, 18, 41-44, 48, 58
doctors (see health)
domestic violence, (see battered women)
doubling up, 55
Drieir, P., xxii, 5-7, 123, 128-129
drop-in centers, 9, 10
drug abuse (see substance abuse)
drug treatment (see substance abuse treatment)
Durbin, J., 126

E

economic conditions, 2-4
education, xv, 41-44, 61, 96, 98, 99, 112, 117, 127, 131, 137
Elsie, 42-43, 53-54, 70, 80, 90-91, 99, 105
emotional status, 65
employment, 14, 18, 48, 50, 57, 59, 62-63, 65, 75-76, 88, 94, 96, 97, 98-99, 117, 121, 127, 131, 138
empowerment, 15, 135, 137
ethnographic research, 16-17, 24-25, 38
eviction (see tenants, landlords)
exercise, 74, 82
exploitation, 112
external validity, 35-36

F

families of origin, 31, 51-54
families of procreation, 31
family, 32, 76-77, 118

family stress, 119
federal housing programs (see subsidized housing)
female-headed household, xxiii, 14-15
feminist research, xi, 135-137
flyers, 27
Fonow, M., 135
food, 67, 76, 77, 78, 79, 101, 112-113, 130, 131, 132-133
foster care, 11
foster parents, 53, 69, 92
Frieda, 30, 31, 43, 54-55, 60, 70, 74-75 80, 83, 94-95
friends, 11, 32, 70-72, 75, 82, 118, 136
funding, 114
future plans, 87-107

G

GA, 4, 42, 54, 62, 75, 102, 121, 129 (see also welfare benefits)
Garret, G., 8
Gayla, 43, 51, 58-59, 61, 68-69, 80-81, 85, 91-92, 95-96, 99, 106
GED, 72, 96, 131
Gilchrist, L., 8
Glaser, B., 24, 33, 34-35, 36
Goering, P., 126
Golden, S., xi-xii
Gottlieb, N., 18
government cutbacks (see cutbacks in social welfare)
Grambs, J., 18
grandchildren, 68-69, 91
grounded theory, 24, 25, 35
group housing, 115

group work, 15-16, 134
Gulf War, 102-103

H
Hagen, J., 13-14
Hamberg, J., xxii-xxiii, 2, 4, 5-6, 8
Hand, J., 16-17
Hanmer, J., 118
Hartman, C., 6
health, 32, 65, 97, 113, 117, 132
Health Care for the Homeless, 36, 50, 58, 113, 126-127
health insurance, 48, 50, 77, 132
Hilda, 43, 48-49, 51, 57, 60-61, 66, 70, 76-77, 81, 92, 96-97, 100
hobbies, 79, 80-81, 82, 85, 95, 97, 99
holidays, 78, 79, 91, 112
Hombs, M, 123
homeless families, xxiii, 8, 11, 17-18
Hooyman, N., 18
Hopper, K., xxi, xxii, xxiii, 1, 2, 4, 5-6, 8-9
housing (see low-income housing)
Huberman, A., 26
HUD, xxii, 6-7, 128
Human Services Strategic Planning Office, xiv
humor, 94, 98
husbands, 41-44

I
illness, 50, 54-55, 60, 72-73, 94
impoverishment (see poverty)
inadequacy, 60

income (see money, wages, low-wage employment)
income maintenance, 117, 129-130 (see also welfare benefits)
inequity, 124
Institute of Medicine, xxii, 1, 5, 8
interviews with women (see data collection)
invisible, xxi
Irene, 43-44, 48-49, 57-58, 66-67, 70, 72, 75-76, 81-82, 92-93, 96
isolation, 115, 118, 119, 126
Ivanoff, A., 13-14

J
Jackie, 44, 50, 82, 93, 101-102
Johnson, A., 13-15, 17-18
Jones, L., 18

K
Karger, H., 2
Katy, 31, 44, 69, 82, 93, 99, 106-107
Katz, M., 3-4, 9
Keefe, T., 1, 11
Keigher, S., xiii
key informants, 36-37
Klein, L., 9
Koegel, P., 16, 24-25
Kozol, J., 5-6
Kreuger, L., 13-15, 17-18
Kutza, E., xiii, 18

L
labor market, 3, 121, 127, 137
landlords, 6, 54-55, 82, 83-85, 133

Lauriet, A., 7
LCC, 26-28, 29, 38, 109-110
Lenin, 103
Levine, T., 9-11
Liebow, E., xi-xiii
limitations, 35-36, 119
loneliness, 120 (see also isolation)
Lopata, H., 18
lovers, 32, 41-44, 48-50, 57-58, 70, 80, 83, 87-88, 90-91, 92, 93, 99, 118, 119
low-income/low-cost housing, xxii, 5-7, 47-48, 102, 113, 117, 122, 123, 126, 127, 128-129, 133, 137-138
lower class, 2
low wage employment, 48, 49, 57, 97, 115, 121, 131

M

manufacturing jobs, 3-4
Marcuse, P., 2-4
Martin, M., 17
Marx, 103
McIntyre, R., 2
Meals on wheels, 133
media, 9
Medicaid, 105, 132
mental health treatment, xv-xvi, 7-8, 9-11, 16, 32, 43-44, 58-59, 66-67, 81, 93, 110, 114, 126-127
mental illness/ mentally ill, xv, 4, 7-8, 9-11, 13-15, 16, 17-18, 26, 43-44, 50, 58-59, 102, 106
Merves, E., 17, 36, 122-123
Miami, 6

middle class, 2, 122-123
Middle East, 123
Milburn, N., xiv
Miles, M., 26
Miller, J., 118
Mississippi, 59-60
Mitchell, J., 120
money, 65, 75, 81, 91, 94, 95, 100, 103, 136
mothers, 59, 80, 101
Multnomah County, 8
myths, xiii, 13, 25

N

National Alliance to End Homelessness, xxii
National Institute of Mental Health (NIMH), 10, 16, 24-25
naturalistic behaviorism, 23
new poor, 12
New York City, 5, 8-9, 16-17, 120
New York State, 93
non-standardized items, 31
normalcy, 44-45, 57-60, 78-82, 98-102, 117, 122-123, 138
Nuccio, K., 18
nutrition, 117, 132-133

O

observation, 37-38
open-ended questions, 31
oppression, 45, 83-85, 107, 124, 125, 136, 137
Oregon, 93
organizing, 16, 83, 85, 138

P
Padachak, D. 126
parents, 53, 69 (also see mothers, foster parents)
part-time jobs, 3, 18, 57
partners (see lovers)
pastimes (see hobbies)
pathways to homelessness, 47-64
patriarchy, xv
Pearce, O., 11
phenomenological research, 23-24, 25
Piven, F., 4
policy implications, 117, 127-133
political awareness, 44-45, 60-63, 82-85, 102-107, 117, 123-124, 136, 138
politics, 102
poor (see poverty)
Portland, OR, 13-14
poverty, 14, 18-19, 45, 47, 48, 61-63, 106, 123, 127, 132, 133
power relations, 3
powerlessness, 125
prison, 42, 52
privacy, 81, 115, 127
protection of human subjects, 39
public housing, (see subsidized housing)
public response, 9, 11-12
public welfare (see welfare benefits)
purposive sampling, 26

Q
qualitative research, xxiv, 16-17, 23-25, 34-35
quantitative research (see cross-sectional surveys)

R
rate of homelessness, xiii, xxi-xxii
Reagan, President, 4, 6, 12, 128
recession, xvii
recruitment, 28-29
reform school, 42, 52
relationships, 44-45, 48-51, 65, 66-72, 87-94, 117, 118-121, 138
relatives, 11
reliability, 34-35
research goals, 21-22
residual approach, 11
resiliency, 44-45, 51-56, 94-98, 117, 121-122, 138
resources, 124, 127, 132 (see also funding)
respect, 112, 113, 124, 127
Ridgeway, J., 4
Roberts, R., 1, 11
Rog, D., 9-11
Roper Organization, 12
Rousseau, A., 12-13, 16
Rubin, L., 7

S
safety, 110, 111, 125, 127
safety net, 138
sample selection, 26-28, 36-37
Schatzman, L., 26, 36
Schonwald, E., 23-24
Scott, H., 5
Section 8, 95, 99
Select Committee on Aging, xiv
selecting shelters, 26-28

Index

selective sampling, 26, 36
self-blame, 60
self-esteem, 96
separation, 18
service providers, xxiv, 26, 35, 52, 71, 72, 113-115, 117, 119, 124-127, 133, 134
service sector jobs, 3
services to the homeless, 8-11, 32, 37, 45, 109-115, 117, 119, 124-127
sexism, 61-63, 85, 133
sexual abuse, 13, 32, 83-84, 90
sharing, 71
shelters, 9, 26-28, 97, 109-115, 126, 129, 138
Shields, L., 18
Shulman, A., 12-13
siblings (see sisters)
single women, 17-18, 19
sisters, 60, 90, 101
skid row, xxi
Slavinsky, A., 8, 13, 119, 121
Smith, S., 13-14, 119
smoking, 109-110
Snyder, M., 123
social benefits (see welfare benefits)
social problem, xxi
Solarz, A., 119-120
Sommers, T., 18
sons, 59, 66-69, 79, 89
spirituality, 113
SRO's, 8, 49, 58, 75-76, 83-85, 93, 94, 102, 120, 133, 134
SSI, 42, 43, 54, 59, 62, 75, 79, 121, 130 (see also welfare benefits)

SSDI, 43, 58, 70, 82, 90, 95, 121, 130
St. Louis, MO, 13-15
Stark, L., 7, 16, 121
Statham, D., 118
staying in contact, 29-30, 38
Stewart B. McKinney Homeless Assistance Act, 10-11
stereotypes, xiii, 66, 78, 118, 121-122
stigma, 106
Stoesz, D., 2
Stoner, M., 8, 13
storage, 96, 99, 101, 126, 127, 129
Strasser, J., 119, 121
Strauss, A., 24, 26, 33, 34-35, 36
structural causes, xv, 119
subgroup, xxiii
subsidized housing, 5-6, 49, 59, 94, 100-101, 102, 107, 127, 128-129, 137
substance abuse, 8, 13-15, 17-18, 26, 32, 41, 43, 49, 58, 66, 67, 76, 77, 88, 114, 136
substance abuse treatment, xv, xvi, 59, 126, 132
Sullivan, M., xii
support system, 32, 45, 93, 119-120
Swanson, J., 34, 35
Swanson-Kauffman, K., 23-24, 25, 33-34
Sweden, 103
symbolic interactionism, 23-24

T

taping, 32, 37
tenants, 54-55, 83-85, 94, 133

Thanksgiving (see holidays)
theoretical sampling, 36
Thomas, W., 36
Toronto, 15
training (see education)
transcripts, 32, 37
transitional housing, 57, 97, 126, 127, 134

U
UI (unemployment insurance), xxiii, 2
unemployment, 2, 48, 122
"unrelated" women, (see single women)
upper class, 2, 58
U.S. Bureau of the Census, xxiv, 2, 19
US Conference of Mayors, xxii

V
validity, 34-35
victimization, 15
violence, 111, 125

W
wages, xv, 122
war, 102-103, 123
Washington DC, 105
wealth, 2
Weatherley, R., xiv, 18
welfare benefits, 18, 48, 114-115, 122, 127, 137
widowhood, 18, 42
witch, xii
Women and Poverty Project, 6
Women's Shelter, 26-28, 37, 85, 109-110, 125, 126
Wright, J., 1, 11-12

Z
Zeifert, M., xii
Znaniecki, F., 36